A-Z COVENTRY

C000114683

From Mary

CONTE...

REFERENCE

Motorway	M6	Car Park (selected)	P
A Road	A46	Church or Chapel	†
B Road	B4098	Cycleway (selected)	
Dual Carriageway		Fire Station	■
One-way Street		Hospital	H
Traffic Flow on A Roads is also indicated by a heavy line on the driver's left.		House Numbers (A & B Roads only)	4 36
Road Under Construction		Information Centre	i
Opening dates are correct at the time of publication.		National Grid Reference	430
Proposed		Park & Ride	Austin Drive P+R
City Centre Ring Road	1	Police Station	▲
Restricted Access		Post Office	★
Pedestrianized Road		Safety Camera with Speed Limit	30
Track or Footpath		Fixed cameras and long term road works cameras. Symbols do not indicate camera direction.	
Railway	Level Crossing / Station / Tunnel	Toilet:	
		without facilities for the Disabled	▽
		with facilities for the Disabled	▽
Built-up Area	HILL ST.	Educational Establishment	■
		Hospital or Healthcare Building	■
Local Authority Boundary		Industrial Building	■
Posttown Boundary		Leisure or Recreational Facility	■
Postcode Boundary (within Posttown)		Place of Interest	■
Map Continuation	10 / Large Scale City Centre 5	Public Building	■
		Shopping Centre or Market	■
Airport	✈	Other Selected Buildings	■

SCALE

Map Pages 6-50	Map Page 4-5
1:15,840 4 inches (10.16 cm) to 1 mile	1:7,920 8 inches (20.32 cm) to 1 mile
0 ¼ ½ Mile	0 ⅛ ¼ Mile
0 250 500 750 Metres	0 100 200 300 Metres
6.31 cm to 1 km	12.63 cm to 1 km

Copyright of Geographers' A-Z Map Company Limited

Fairfield Road, Borough Green, Sevenoaks, Kent TN15 8PP
Telephone: 01732 781000 (Enquiries & Trade Sales)
01732 783422 (Retail Sales)
www.az.co.uk
Copyright © Geographers' A-Z Map Co. Ltd.
Edition 6 2013

Every possible care has been taken to ensure that, to the best of our knowledge, the information contained in this atlas is accurate at the date of publication. However, we cannot warrant that our work is entirely error free and whilst we would be grateful to learn of any inaccuracies, we do not accept any responsibility for loss or damage resulting from reliance on information contained within this publication.

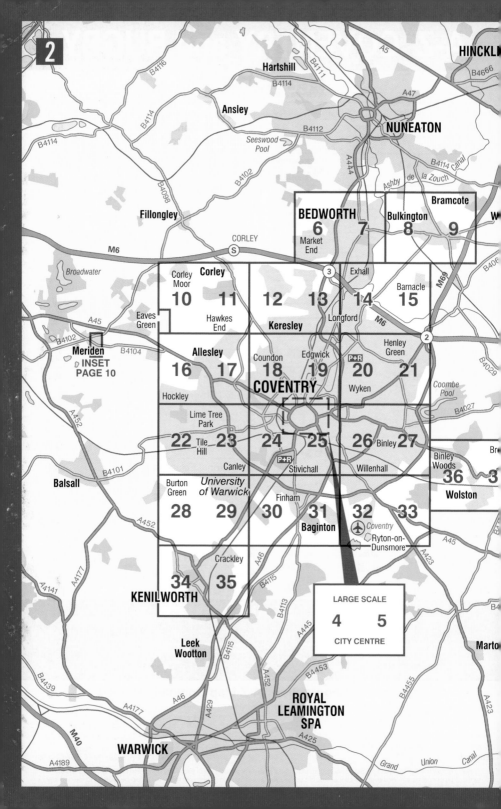

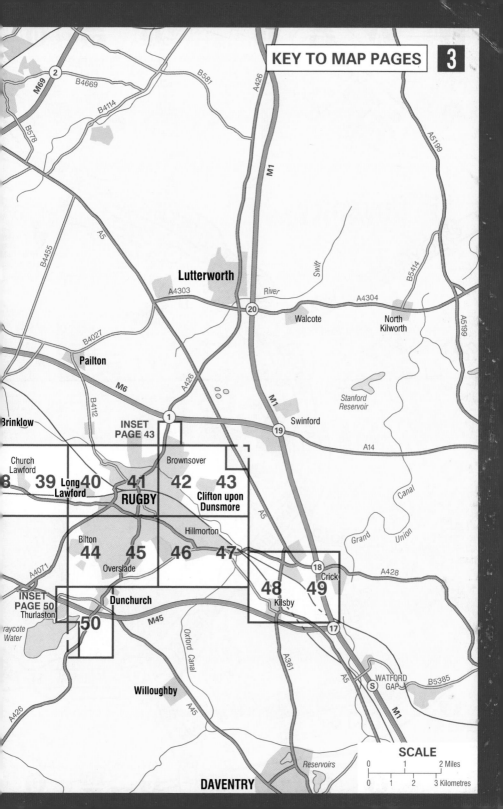

M69
B4669
B4114
B578
B4455
B581
A426
B4027
A5199
M1
Lutterworth
A4303
Swift
River
A4304
B5414
Walcote
North Kilworth
A5199
Pailton
M6
A426
B4112
Stanford Reservoir
Brinklow
INSET PAGE 43
1
M1
19
Swinford
A14
Church Lawford
Brownsover
Canal
8 39 Long Lawford 40 41 42 43
RUGBY
Clifton upon Dunsmore
Bilton
Hillmorton
Grand
Union
44 45 46 47
Overslade
18
Crick
A428
A4071
48 49
Kilsby
A5
INSET PAGE 50
Thurlaston
Dunchurch
50
M45
17
raycote Water
Oxford Canal
A361
WATFORD GAP
S
B5385
Willoughby
A45
A426
M1

SCALE

0		1		2 Miles
0	1	2		3 Kilometres

Reservoirs
DAVENTRY

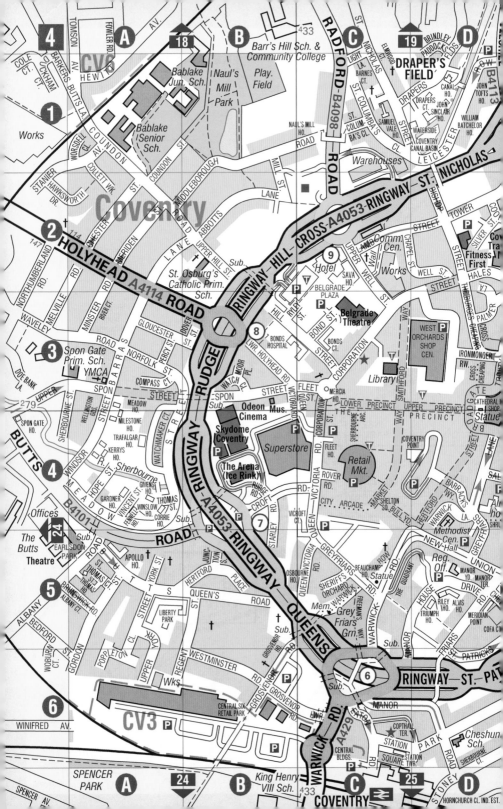

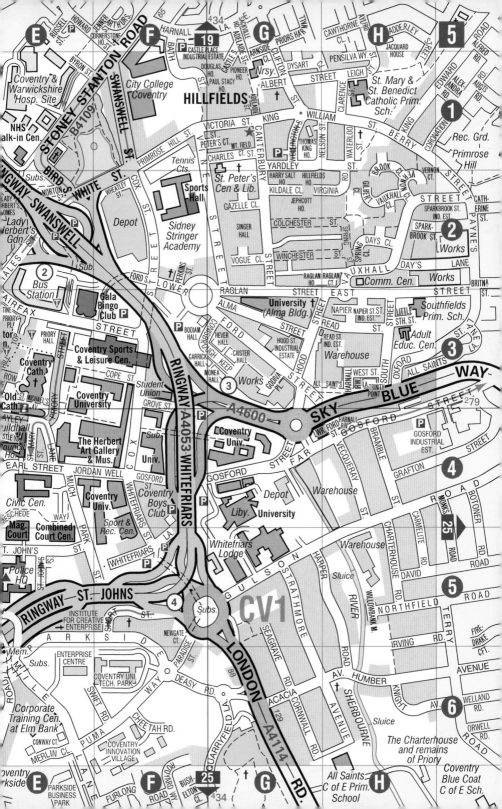

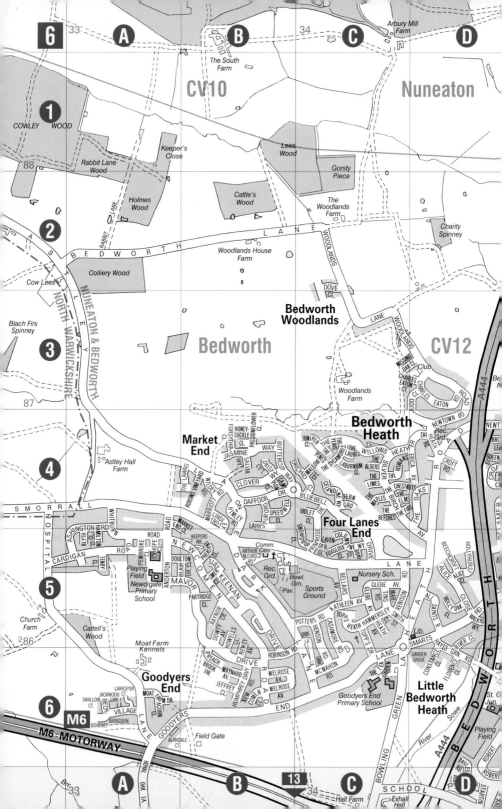

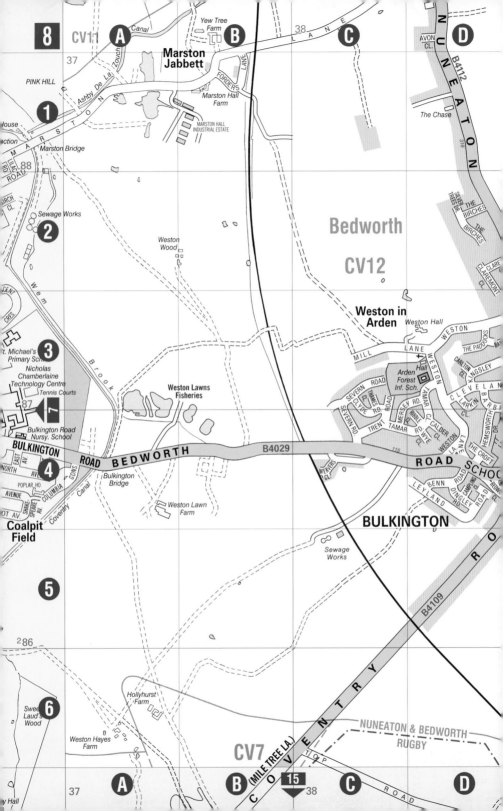

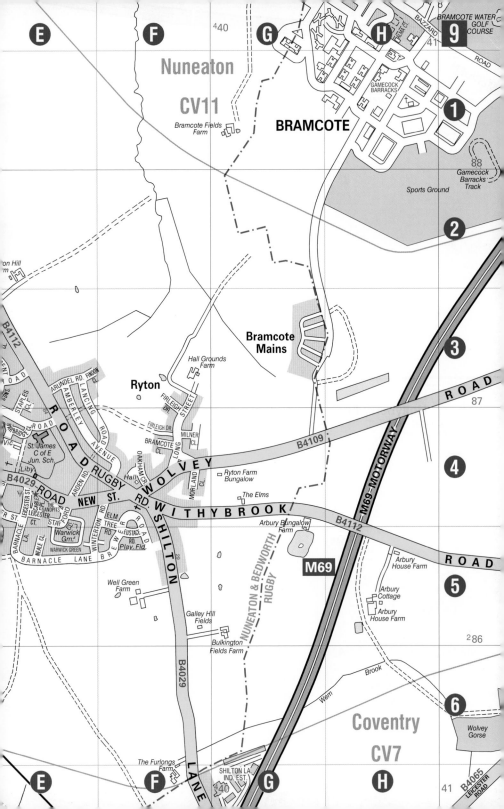

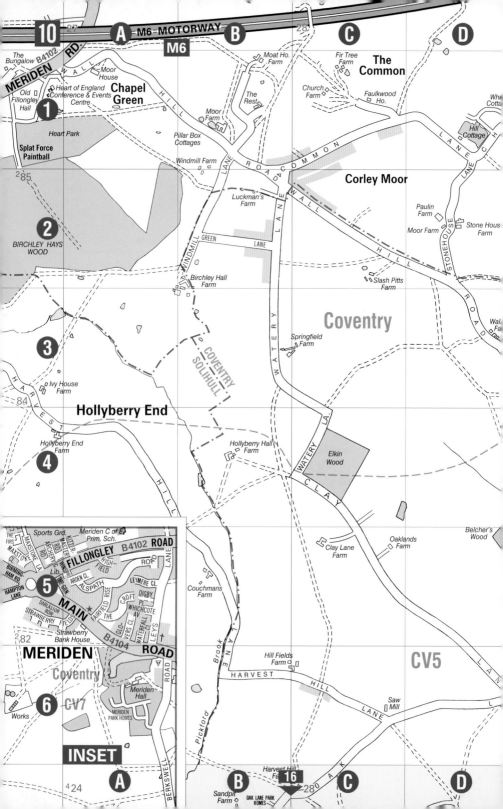

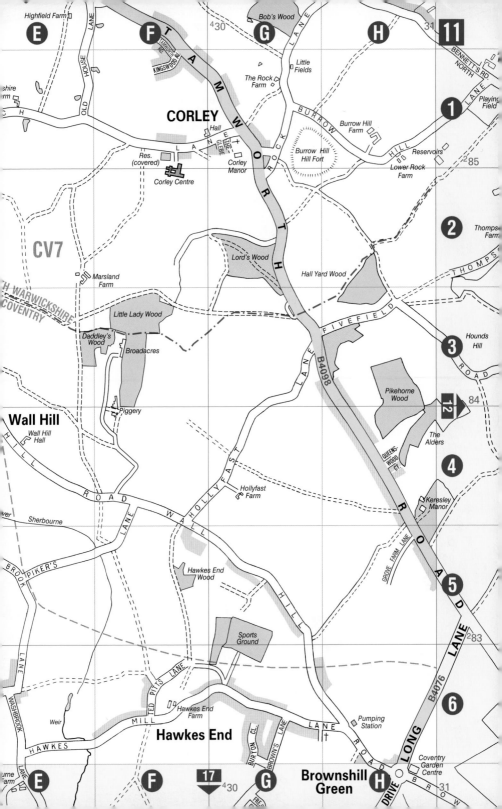

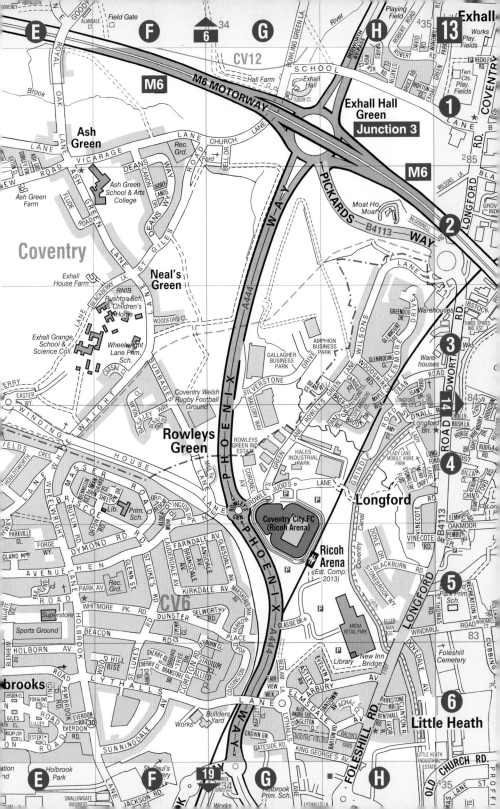

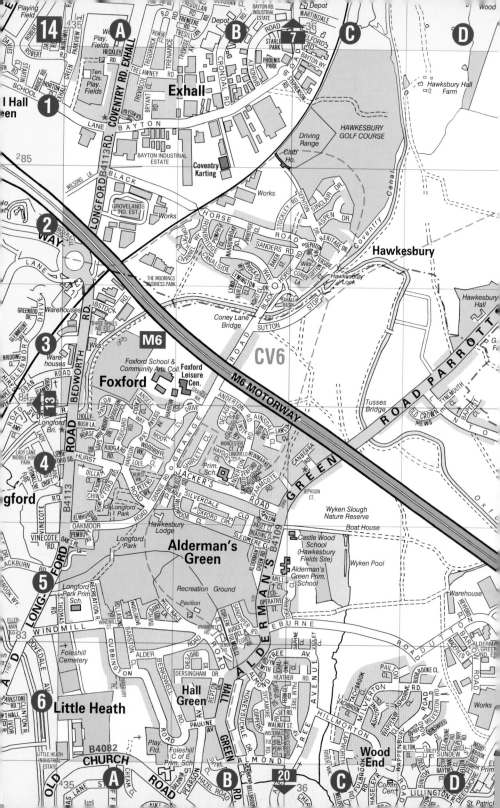

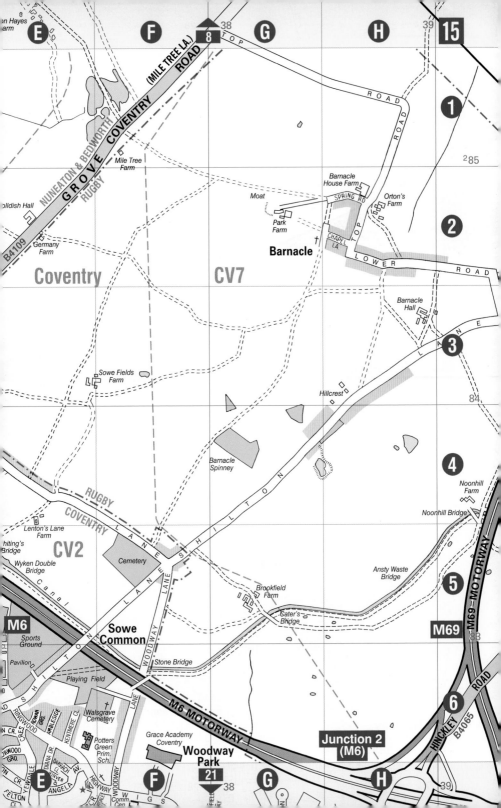

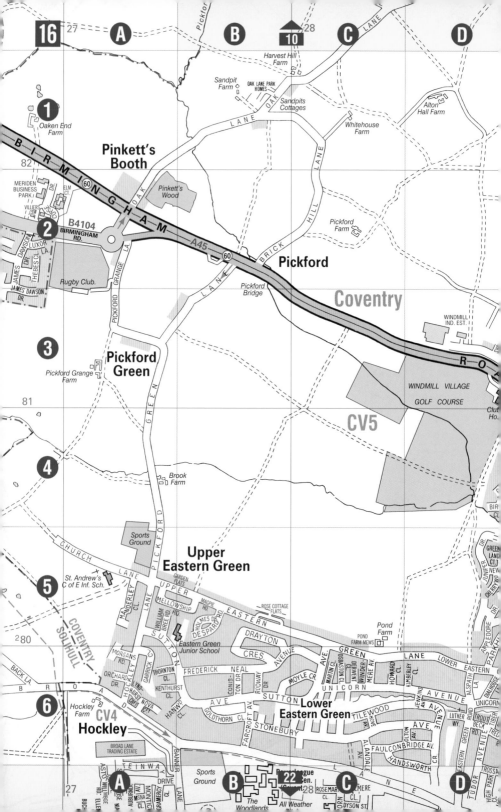

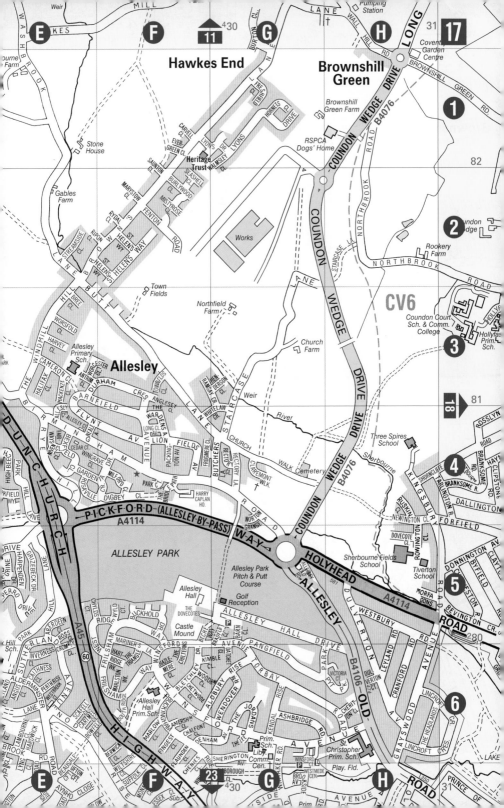

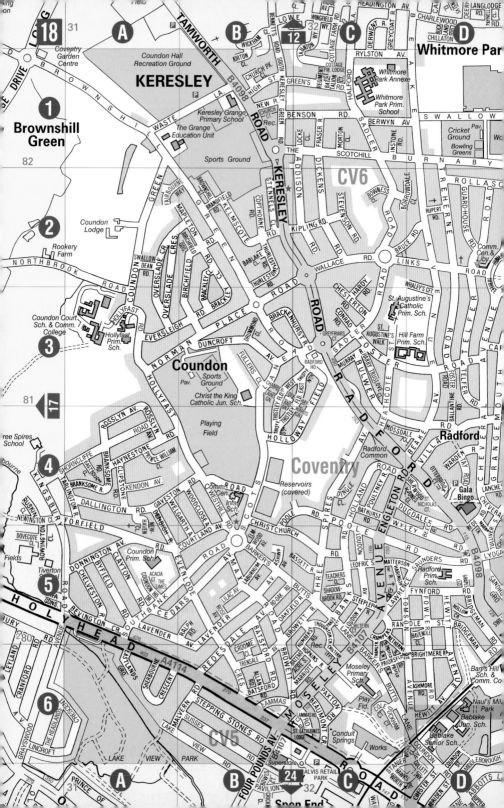

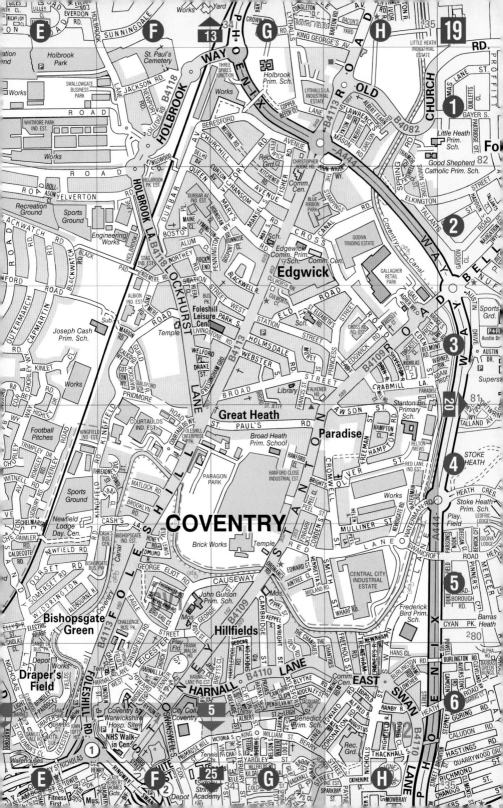

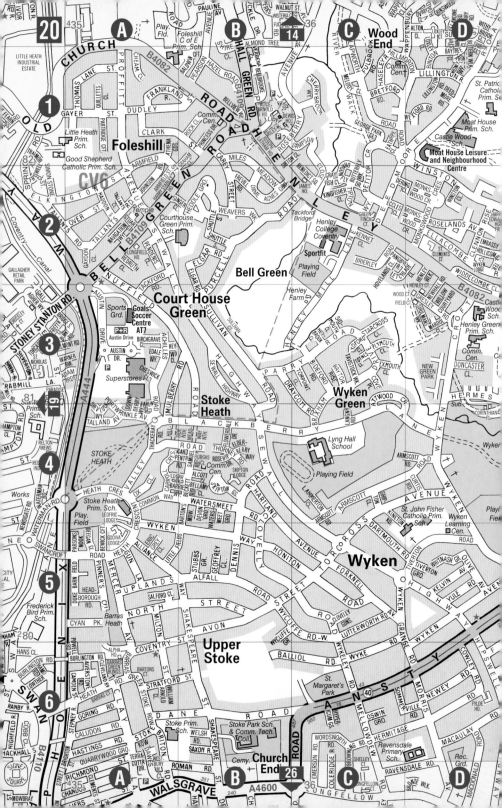

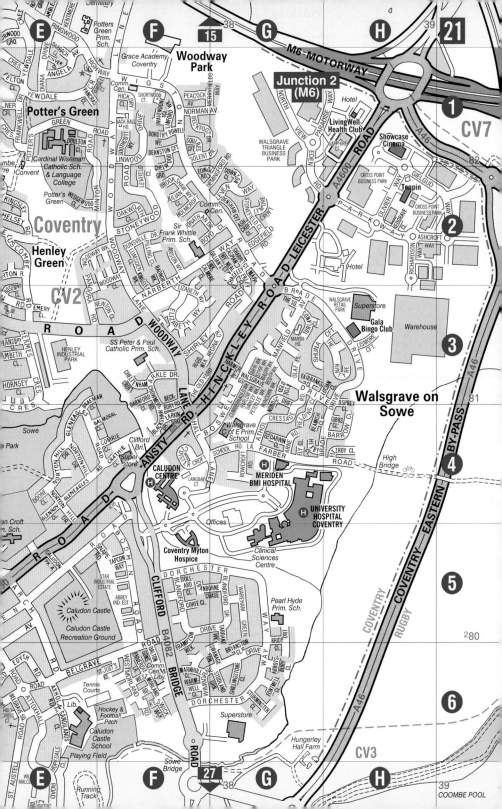

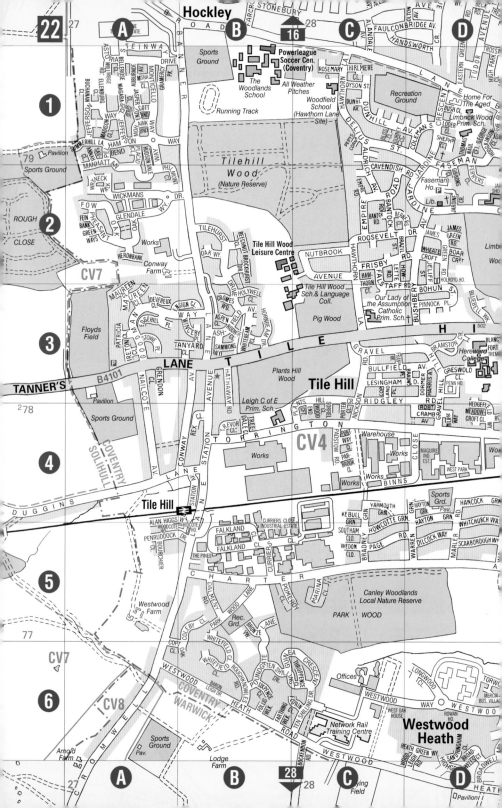

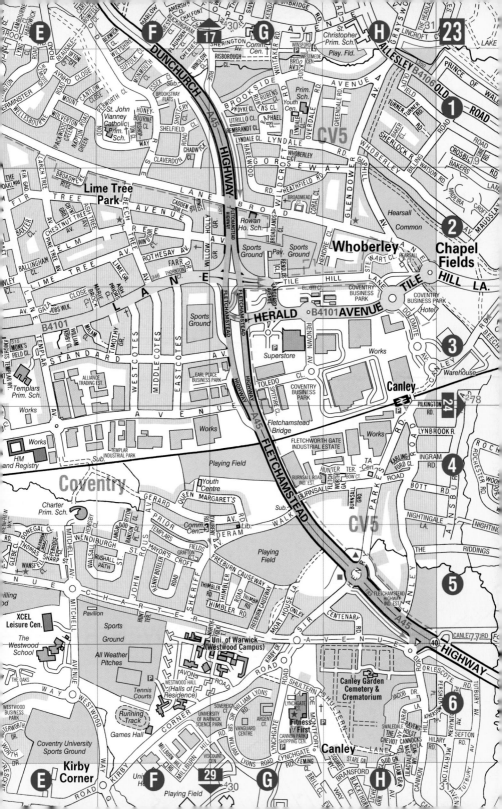

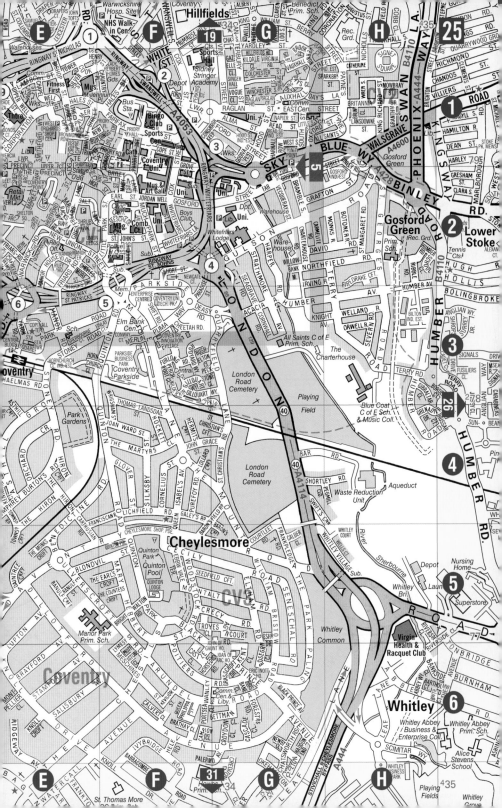

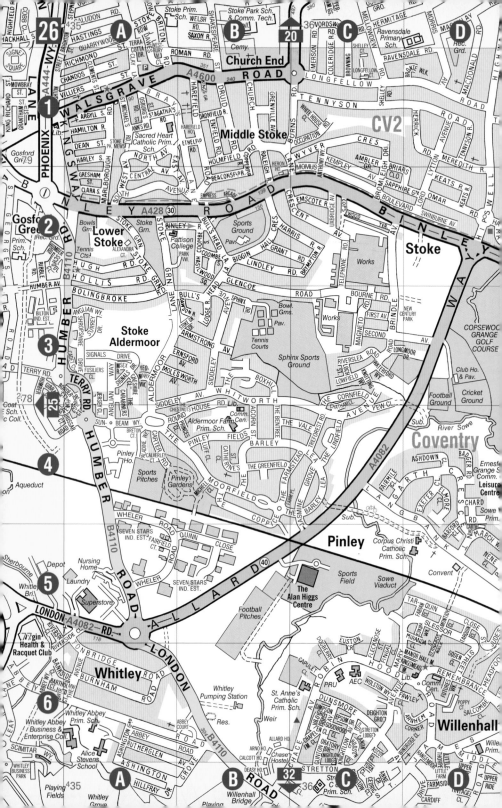

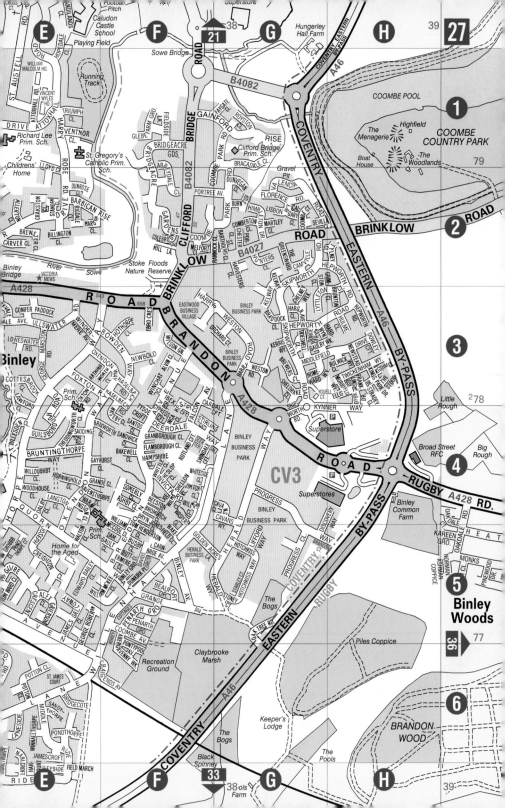

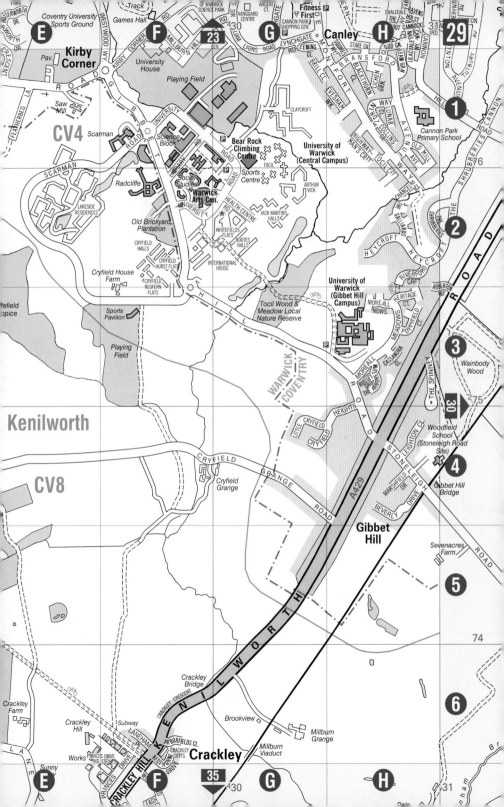

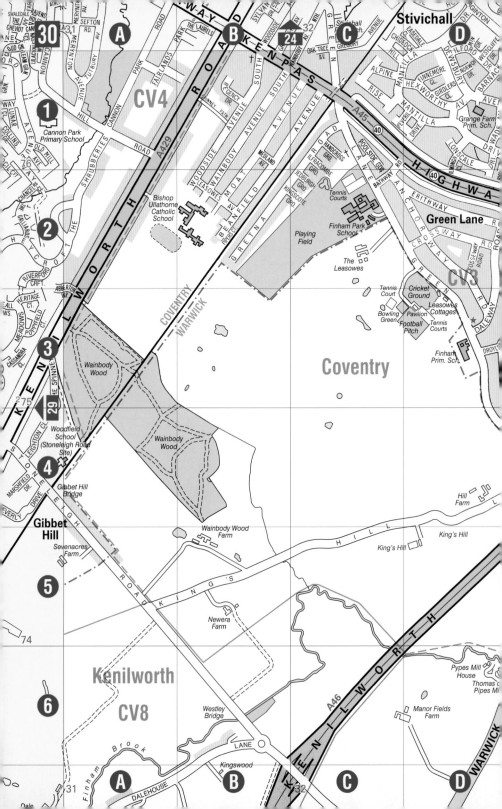

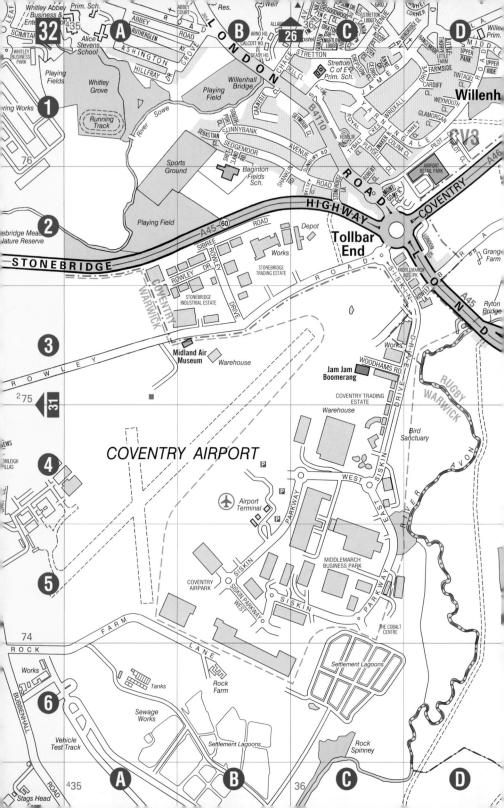

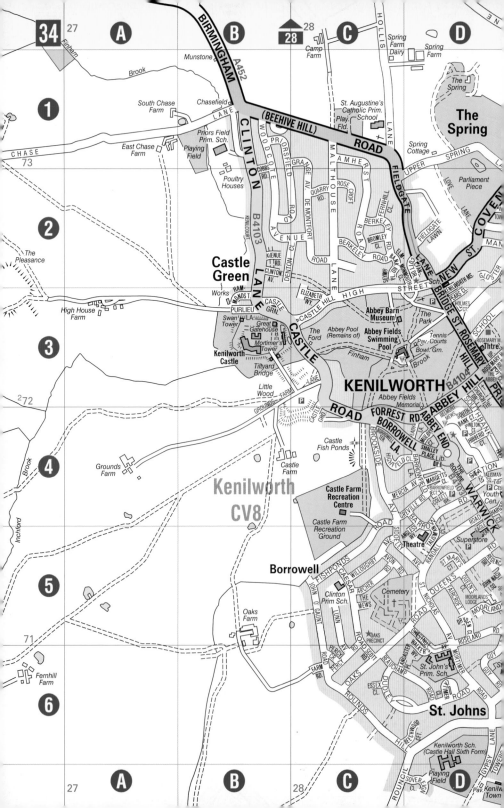

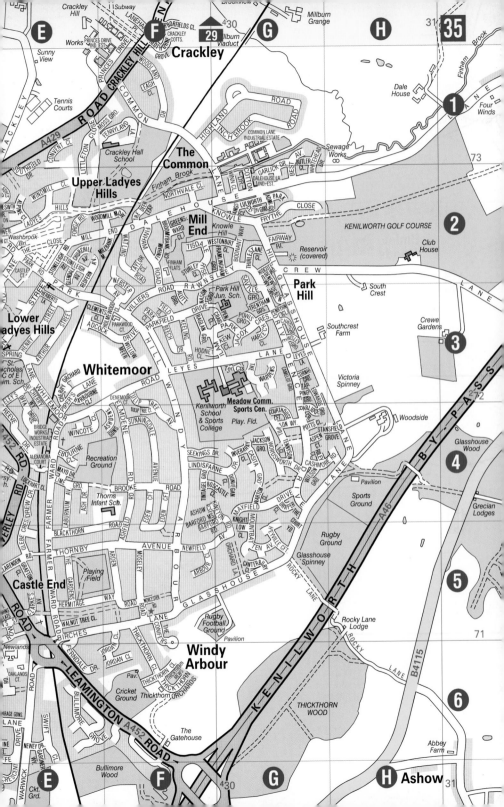

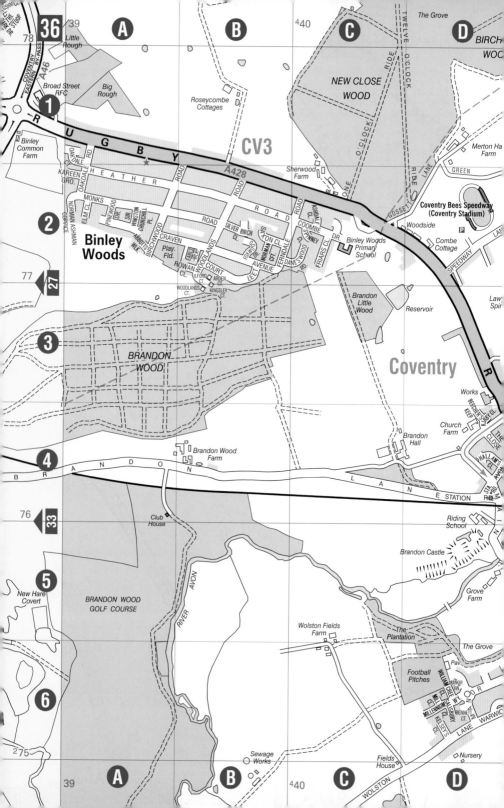

A   B   440   C   D

Little Rough

78

BIRCH WOO

The Grove

NEW CLOSE WOOD

Broad Street RFC

Big Rough

Roseycombe Cottages

1

CV3

Merton Ha Farm

Binley Common Farm

OAKDALE RD.

KAREEN GRO.

HEATHER

A428

Sherwood Farm

Woodside

GREEN

Coventry Bees Speedway (Coventry Stadium)

MONKS

PINEWOOD DR.

ELM CL.

NORMAN ASHMAN COPPICE

2

SIR WINSTON CHURCHILL PL.

BIRCHWOOD

ABBOTTS WLK.

CRAVEN

Play. Fld.

ROAD

SILVER BIRCH

SIXTON CL.

NORMAN CFT.

FERNDALE DR.

COOMBE

DANESWOOD RD.

FRIARS CL.

PINNEY CL.

Binley Woods Priman School

Combe Cottage

Binley Woods

ROWAN CL.

WOODLANDS COURT

ILFORD CT.

ARDEN CT.

KINGSLEY CT.

WOODLANDS CT.

AVENUE

LEET

Brandon Little Wood

Reservoir

Law Spir

77 **27**

Coventry

3

BRANDON WOOD

Works

BEECHER'S CL.

RUGBY CL.

KEEP CL.

Church Farm

THE CLOSE

4

B R A N D O N   L A N E STATION RD.

Brandon Wood Farm

Brandon Hall

HALLAM CL.

STA RD.

MAIN

76 **33**

Club House

Riding School

Brandon Castle

Grove Farm

5

New Hare Covert

BRANDON WOOD GOLF COURSE

RIVER AVON

Wolston Fields Farm

The Plantation

The Grove

Pav

6

Football Pitches

WILLIAM TREE WY.

MANOR WY.

ASBURY CT.

MILLENNIUM CT.

BENNETT CT.

KELSEY'S CL.

275

39   A   B   440   C   WOLSTON LANE   WARWIC   D

Fields House

Sewage Works

Nursery

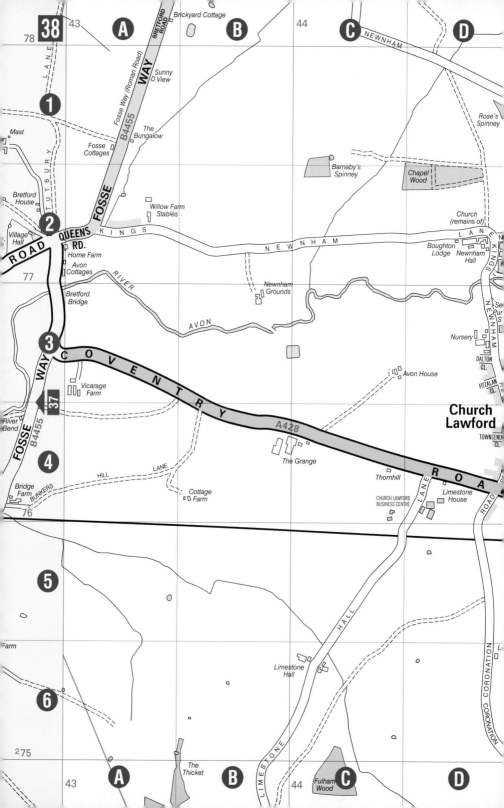

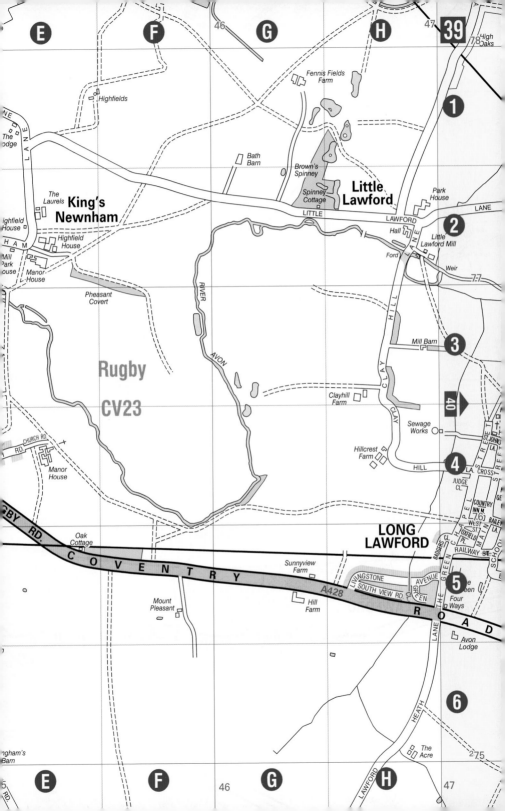

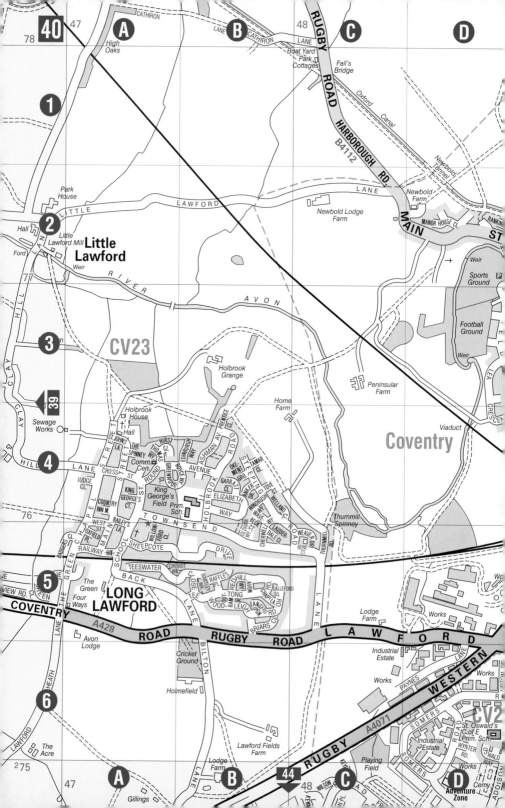

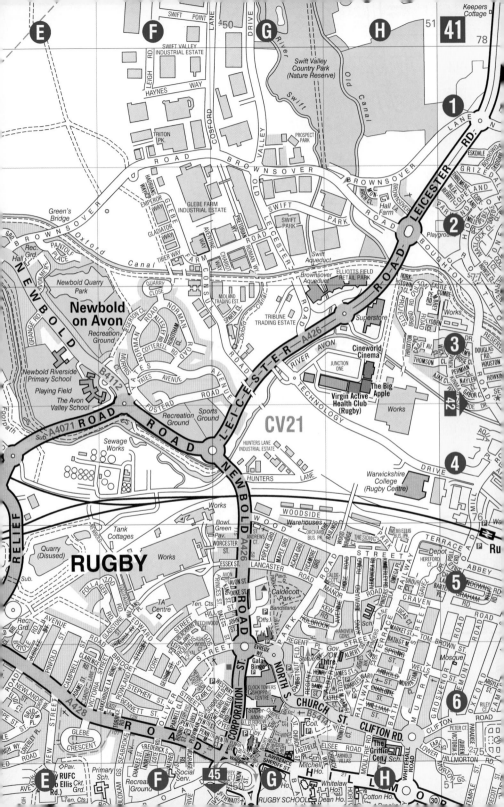

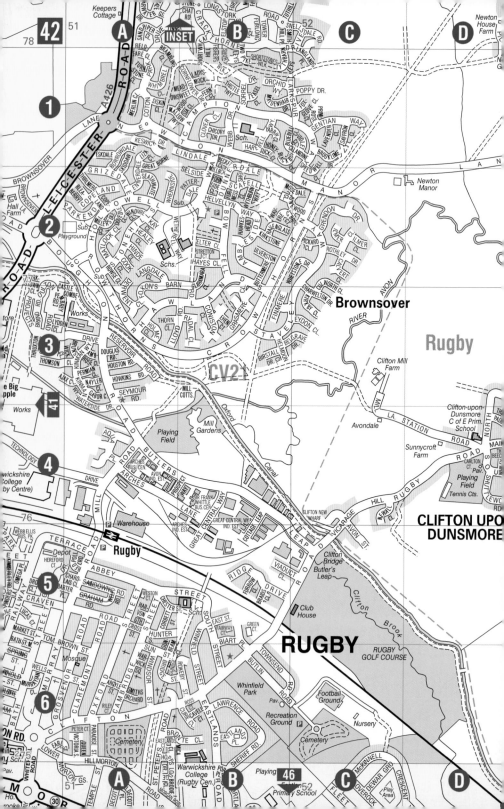

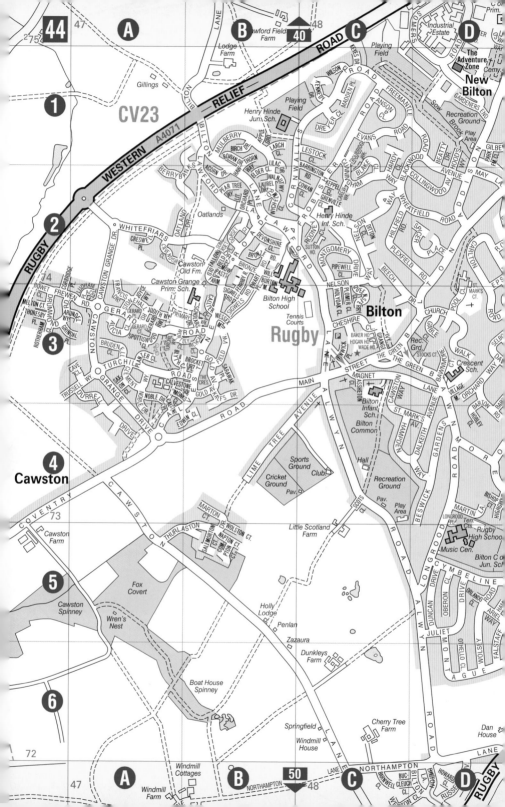

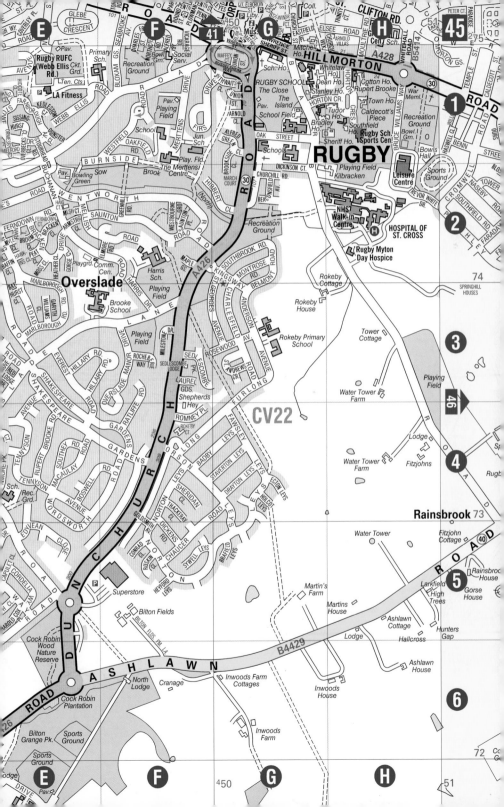

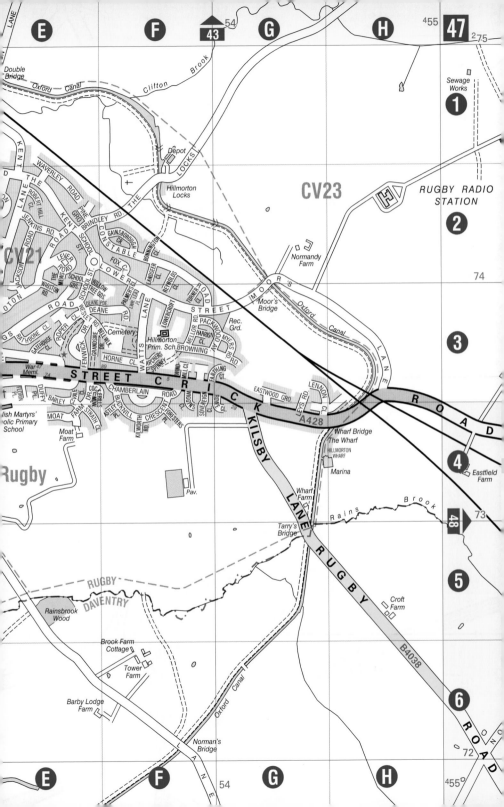

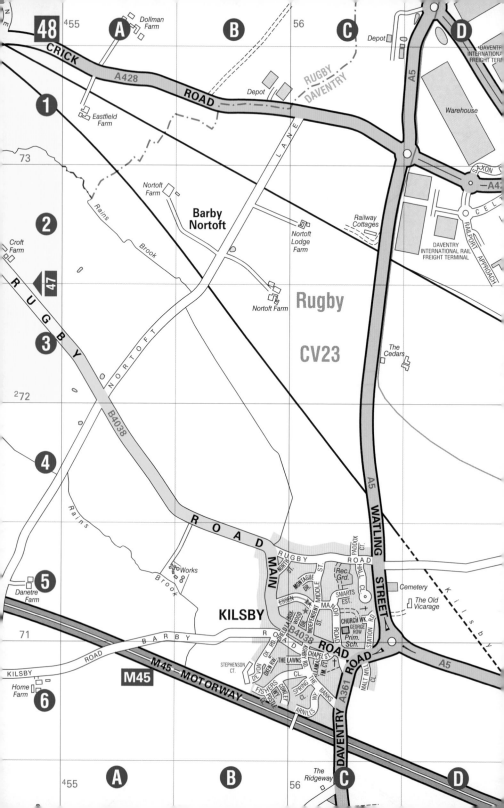

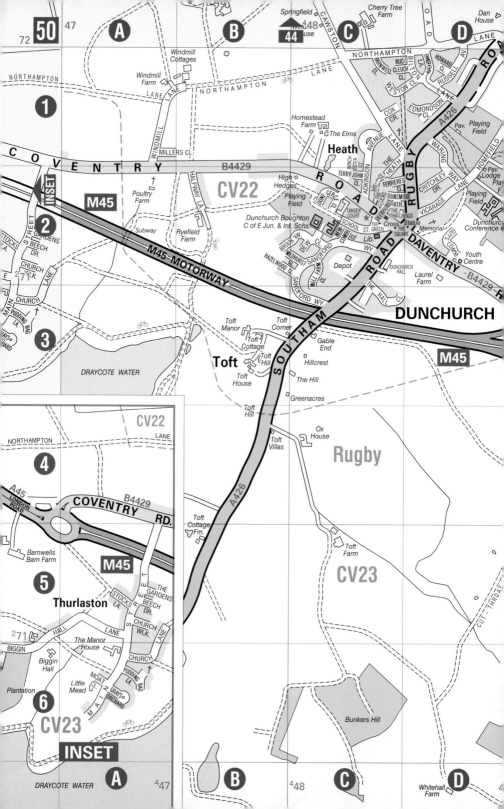

INDEX

Including Streets, Places & Areas, Hospitals etc., Industrial Estates,
Selected Flats & Walkways, Stations and Selected Places of Interest.

HOW TO USE THIS INDEX

1. Each street name is followed by its Postcode District, then by its Locality abbreviation(s) and then by its map reference;
e.g. **Abbey Hill** CV8: Ken . . . .3D **34** is in the CV8 Postcode District and the Kenilworth Locality and is to be found in square 3D on page **34**. The page number is shown in bold type.

2. A strict alphabetical order is followed in which Av., Rd., St., etc. (though abbreviated) are read in full and as part of the street name; e.g. **Ash Ct.** appears after **Ashcombe Dr.** but before **Ashcroft Cl.**

3. Street and a selection of flats and walkways that cannot be shown on the mapping, appear in the index with the thoroughfare to which they are connected shown in brackets; **Alderman Gee Hall** CV12: Bed . . . .2E **7** (off Newdigate Rd.)

4. Addresses that are in more than one part are referred to as not continuous.

5. Places and areas are shown in the index in BLUE TYPE and the map reference is to the actual map square in which the town centre or area is located and not to the place name shown on the map; e.g. **BEDWORTH** 4F **7**

6. An example of a selected place of interest is Abbey Barn Mus. 3C **34**

7. An example of a station is Bedworth Station (Rail) . . . .4G **7**, also included is Park & Ride. e.g. **Austin Drive (Park & Ride)** 3A **20**

8. An example of a Hospital, Hospice or selected Healthcare facility is HOSPITAL OF ST CROSS 2H **45**

9. Map references for entries that appear on large scale pages **4** & **5** are shown first, with small scale map references shown in brackets; e.g. **Abbotts La.** CV1: Cov 2B **4** (1D **24**)

GENERAL ABBREVIATIONS

App. : Approach	**Cres.** : Crescent	**Ind.** : Industrial	**Pct.** : Precinct
Arc. : Arcade	**Cft.** : Croft	**Info.** : Information	**Ri.** : Rise
Av. : Avenue	**Dr.** : Drive	**Intl.** : International	**Rd.** : Road
Blvd. : Boulevard	**E.** : East	**Junc.** : Junction	**Shop.** : Shopping
Bri. : Bridge	**Ent.** : Enterprise	**La.** : Lane	**Sth.** : South
Bldgs. : Buildings	**Est.** : Estate	**Lit.** : Little	**Sq.** : Square
Bungs. : Bungalows	**Fld.** : Field	**Lwr.** : Lower	**St.** : Street
Bus. : Business	**Flds.** : Fields	**Mnr.** : Manor	**Ter.** : Terrace
C'way. : Causeway	**Gdn.** : Garden	**Mans.** : Mansions	**Twr.** : Tower
Cen. : Centre	**Gdns.** : Gardens	**Mdw.** : Meadow	**Trad.** : Trading
Chyd. : Churchyard	**Gth.** : Garth	**Mdws.** : Meadows	**Up.** : Upper
Circ. : Circle	**Ga.** : Gate	**M.** : Mews	**Va.** : Vale
Cl. : Close	**Gt.** : Great	**Mt.** : Mount	**Vw.** : View
Comn. : Common	**Grn.** : Green	**Mus.** : Museum	**Vs.** : Villas
Cnr. : Corner	**Gro.** : Grove	**Nth.** : North	**Vis.** : Visitors
Cott. : Cottage	**Hgts.** : Heights	**Pde.** : Parade	**Wlk.** : Walk
Cotts. : Cottages	**Ho.** : House	**Pk.** : Park	**W.** : West
Ct. : Court	**Ho's.** : Houses	**Pl.** : Place	**Yd.** : Yard

LOCALITY ABBREVIATIONS

Ald G : **Alderman's Green**	**Brin** : **Brinklow**	**Exh** : **Exhall**	**Milli W** : **Millison's Wood**
Alle : **Allesley**	**Brow** : **Brownsover**	**Fill** : **Fillongley**	**N'bld A** : **Newbold on Avon**
Ansty : **Ansty**	**Bubb** : **Bubbenhall**	**Finh** : **Finham**	**Newt** : **Newton**
Ash G : **Ash Green**	**Bulk** : **Bulkington**	**Griff** : **Griff**	**Nun** : **Nuneaton**
Ashow : **Ashow**	**Burt G** : **Burton Green**	**Harb M** : **Harborough Magna**	**Rugby** : **Rugby**
Bag : **Baginton**	**Canly** : **Canley**	**Harb P** : **Harborough Parva**	**Rytn D** : **Ryton-on-Dunsmore**
Barby : **Barby**	**Cath** : **Cathiron**	**Hillm** : **Hillmorton**	**Shilt** : **Shilton**
Barn : **Barnacle**	**Caw** : **Cawston**	**Ken** : **Kenilworth**	**S'lgh** : **Stoneleigh**
Bed : **Bedworth**	**Chu L** : **Church Lawford**	**Ker E** : **Keresley End**	**Thurl** : **Thurlaston**
Berk : **Berkswell**	**Clift D** : **Clifton upon Dunsmore**	**Kils** : **Kilsby**	**Tile H** : **Tile Hill**
Bil : **Bilton**	**Cor** : **Corley**	**King New** : **King's Newnham**	**Walsg S** : **Walsgrave on Sowe**
Bin : **Binley**	**Cosf** : **Cosford**	**Law H** : **Lawford Heath**	**Westw H** : **Westwood Heath**
Bin W : **Binley Woods**	**Crick** : **Crick**	**Lit L** : **Little Lawford**	**W'hall** : **Willenhall**
Bram : **Bramcote**	**Dunc** : **Dunchurch**	**Longf** : **Longford**	**Withy** : **Withybrook**
Bran : **Brandon**	**E Grn** : **Eastern Green**	**Long L** : **Long Lawford**	**Wols** : **Wolston**
Bret : **Bretford**		**Mer** : **Meriden**	**Wool** : **Woolscott**

A

Abberton Way CV4: Canly . . .3H **29**	**Abingdon** CV12: Bed 6A **6**	**Agincourt Rd.** CV3: Cov 5G **25**
Abbey, The CV8: Ken 3D **34**	**Acacia Av.** CV1: Cov 6G **5** (3G **25**)	**Ainsbury Rd.** CV5: Cov 4A **24**
Abbey Barn Mus. 3C **34**	**Acacia Cl.** CV6: Cov 5A **18**	**Ainsdale Cl.** CV6: Ald G 4B **14**
Abbey Cl. CV3: Bin 5F **27**	**Acacia Cres.** CV12: Bed 3H **7**	**Aintree Cl.** CV6: Cov 5G **19**
Abbey Cotts. CV3: Bin 5F **27**	**Acacia Gro.** CV21: Rugby 5G **41**	CV12: Bed 2F **7**
Abbey Ct. CV3: Cov 6B **26**	**Achal Cl.** CV6: Cov 6H **13**	**Airport Retail Pk.** CV3: W'hall . . .1D **32**
Abbeydale Cl. CV3: Bin 1F **27**	**Achilles Rd.** CV6: Cov 3A **20**	**Ajax Cl.** CV21: Rugby 3H **41**
Abbey End CV8: Ken 4D **34**	**Acorn Cl.** CV12: Bed 6A **6**	**Alandale Av.** CV5: E Grn 6C **16**
Abbey Fields Swimming Pool . .3C **34**	**Acorn Dr.** CV22: Bil 2B **44**	**Alandale Ct.** CV12: Bed 6A **6**
Abbey Hill CV8: Ken 3D **34**	**Acorn St.** CV3: Cov 4B **26**	**Alan Higgs Centre, The** 5C **26**
Abbey Ind. Est. CV2: Cov 5F **21**	**Adam Rd.** CV6: Cov 3A **20**	**Alan Higgs Way** CV4: Tile H 4A **22**
Abbey Rd. CV3: Cov 6H **25**	**Adams St.** CV21: Rugby 6E **41**	**Alan Marcell Cl.** CV4: Tile H 4E **23**
(not continuous)	**Adare Dr.** CV3: Cov 4E **25**	**Albany Cl.** CV1: Cov 5A **4** (2C **24**)
Abbey St. CV21: Rugby 5A **42**	**Adcock Dr.** CV8: Ken 3E **35**	**Albany Rd.** CV1: Cov 5A **4** (3C **24**)
Abbey Way CV3: Cov 6H **25**	**Addenbrooke Rd.**	CV5: Cov 3C **24**
Abbotsbury Cl. CV2: Walsg S . . .6G **21**	CV7: Ker E 2C **12**	**Albert Cres.** CV6: Cov 5D **12**
Abbotts La. CV1: Cov 2B **4** (1D **24**)	**Adderley St.** CV1: Cov . . .1H **5** (6G **19**)	**Albert Fearn Gdns.** CV6: Cov 1H **19**
Abbotts Wlk. CV3: Bin W 2A **36**	**Addison Rd.** CV6: Cov 2C **18**	**Albert Sq.** CV21: Rugby 6H **41**
CV8: Wols 5F **37**	CV22: Bil, Rugby 2D **44**	**Albert St.** CV1: Cov 1G **5** (6G **19**)
Abbotts Way CV21: Hillm 2D **46**	**Adelaide Ct.** CV12: Bed 4D **6**	CV21: Rugby 6H **41**
Abercorn Rd. CV5: Cov 2A **24**	**Adelaide St.** CV1: Cov . .1G **5** (6G **19**)	**Albion Ind. Est.** CV6: Cov 3F **19**
Aberdeen Cl. CV5: E Grn 5E **17**	(not continuous)	**Albion St.** CV8: Ken 3E **35**
Abergavenny Wlk. CV3: Bin 5F **27**	**Adkinson Av.** CV22: Dunc 2C **50**	**Alcott Cl.** CV2: Cov 4B **20**
	Admiral Gdns. CV8: Ken 2G **35**	**Aldbourne Rd.** CV1: Cov 5E **19**
	Adventure Zone, The 1D **44**	**Aldbury Ri.** CV5: Cov 6F **17**

Alderman Gee Hall CV12: Bed 2E **7**
(off Newdigate Rd.)
ALDERMAN'S GREEN 5B **14**
Alderman's Grn. Ind. Est.
CV2: Ald G 5D **14**
Alderman's Grn. Rd.
CV2: Ald G 6B **14**
(not continuous)
Alder Mdw. Cl. CV6: Cov 4F **13**
Alderminster Rd. CV5: E Grn 6E **17**
Aldermoor La. CV3: Cov 3A **26**
Alderney Cl. CV6: Cov 6D **12**
Alder Rd. CV6: Cov 6A **14**
Alders, The CV12: Bed 4C **6**
Aldrich Av. CV4: Tile H 1C **22**
Aldrin Way CV4: Canly 1H **29**
Alec Wilson Sports Cen. 2F **7**
Alexander Rd. CV12: Bed 3G **7**
Alexandra Ct. CV3: Cov 2A **26**
CV8: Ken 4E **35**
CV21: Rugby 6H **41**
(off Charles Warren Cl.)
Alexandra Rd.
CV1: Cov 1H **5** (6H **19**)
CV21: Rugby 6H **41**

Alexandra Ter.—Beckfoot Cl.

Alexandra Ter. CV6: Cov 6G **13**
Alexandra Wlk. *CV21: Rugby 6H **41***
(off Charles Warren Cl.)
Alex Grierson Cl. CV3: Bin 5E **27**
Alfall Rd. CV2: Cov 5B **20**
Alfred Grn. Cl. CV22: Rugby 1G **45**
Alfred Rd. CV1: Cov 1H **5** (6H **19**)
Alfred St. CV21: Rugby 6F **41**
Alfriston Rd. CV3: Finh 2E **31**
Algate Cl. CV6: Cov 5E **13**
Alice Arnold Ho. CV2: Cov 1B **20**
Alice Cl. CV12: Bed 5D **6**
Alice Ct. NN6: Crick 2H **49**
Alicia Cl. CV22: Caw 3A **44**
Alison Sq. CV2: Ald G 4B **14**
Allan Rd. CV6: Cov 6B **18**
Allans Cl. CV23: Clift D 4E **43**
Allans Dr. CV23: Clift D 4E **43**
Allans La. CV23: Clift D 4E **43**
Allard Ho. CV3: W'hall 6B **26**
Allard Way CV3: Bin, Cov 5A **26**
Allerton Cl. CV2: Cov 2E **27**
Allerton Rd. CV23: Brow 2H **43**
ALLESLEY 3E **17**
Allesley By-Pass
CV5: Alle, Cov 4F **17**
Allesley Ct. CV5: Alle 4E **17**
Allesley Cft. CV5: Alle 4E **17**
Allesley Hall Dr.
CV5: Alle, Cov 5G **17**
Allesley Old Rd. CV5: Cov 5G **17**
Allesley Park Pitch & Putt Course
5G **17**
Allesley Rd. CV21: N'bld A 3F **41**
Alliance Trad. Est. CV4: Tile H 3E **23**
Alliance Way CV2: Cov 5A **20**
Allied Cl. CV6: Cov 6F **13**
Allitt Gro. CV8: Ken 3F **35**
All Saints La. CV1: Cov 3G **5**
(Lwr. Ford St.)
CV1: Cov 3H **5** (1G **25**)
(Oxford St.)
All Saints Rd. CV12: Bed 5D **6**
All Saints Sq. CV12: Bed 3F **7**
Alma Ct. CV11: Bram 1H **9**
Alma St. CV1: Cov 3G **5** (1G **25**)
Almond Gro. CV21: N'bld A 2E **41**
Almond Tree Av. CV2: Cov 6B **14**
Almshouses CV12: Bed 3G **7**
Alpha Bus. Pk. CV2: Cov 1D **20**
Alpha Ho. CV2: Cov 6A **20**
Alpine Ct. CV8: Ken 2E **35**
Alpine Ri. CV3: Cov 1C **30**
Alspath La. CV5: E Grn 6D **16**
Alspath Rd. CV7: Mer 5A **10**
Alton Cl. CV2: Cov 6D **14**
Alum Cl. CV6: Cov 2F **19**
Alverley Rd. CV6: Cov 4E **19**
Alverstone Rd. CV2: Cov 6A **20**
Alvin Cl. CV3: Bin 3F **27**
Alvis Ho. CV1: Cov 5D **4**
Alvis Retail Pk. CV5: Cov 1C **24**
Alvyn Smith Cl. CV2: Cov 6B **14**
Alwyn Freeman Ct. *CV7: Ker E 2C **12***
(off Somers Rd.)
Alwyn Rd. CV22: Bil 3C **44**
Amberley Av. CV12: Bulk 3E **9**
Ambler Gro. CV2: Cov 1C **26**
Ambleside CV2: Walsg S 6E **15**
CV21: Brow 2B **42**
Ambleside Rd. CV12: Bed 4E **7**
Ambrose Cl. CV21: Rugby 3A **42**
Amelia Cl. CV12: Bulk 3E **9**
Amersham Cl. CV5: Cov 6F **17**
Amherst Rd. CV8: Ken 1C **34**
Amos Jacques Rd. CV12: Bed 2E **7**
Amphion Bus. Pk. CV6: Ash G 3G **13**
Amy Cl. CV6: Longf 4H **13**
Anchorway Rd. CV3: Finh 2C **30**
Anderson Av. CV22: Rugby 3G **45**
Anderton Rd. CV6: Ald G 3B **14**
CV12: Bed 5A **6**
Andrews Cl. CV8: Bag 4H **31**
Angela Av. CV2: Walsg S 1E **21**
Anglesey Cl. CV5: Alle 3F **17**
Angless Way CV8: Ken 5D **34**
Anglian Way CV3: Cov 3A **26**
(not continuous)
Angus Cl. CV5: E Grn 6E **17**
CV8: Ken 2G **35**
Anker Dr. CV23: Long L 4B **40**
Anley Way CV6: Cov 4E **19**
Anne Cres. CV3: W'hall 1C **32**
Ansell Dr. CV6: Longf 3A **14**
Anson Cl. CV22: Bil 1C **44**
Anson Way CV2: Walsg S 2F **21**
Ansty Rd. CV2: Cov 6C **20**
CV2: Walsg S 4F **21**
Anthony Way CV2: Cov 2C **26**
Antrim Cl. CV5: Alle 3E **17**
Apollo Ho. CV1: Cov 5A **4** (2D **24**)
Applecross Cl. CV4: Westw H 6D **22**
Appledore Dr. CV5: Alle 5D **16**
Apple Gro. CV22: Bil 1B **44**
Appleyard Cl. CV12: Bed 4F **7**
Aqua Pl. CV21: Rugby 4A **42**
Arboretum, The CV4: Canly 3H **29**
Arborfields Cl. CV8: Ken 6F **29**
Arbour Cl. CV8: Ken 5F **35**
CV22: Rugby 4D **44**
Arbours, The CV22: Rugby 1A **46**
Arbury Av. CV6: Cov 6G **13**
CV12: Bed 3E **7**
Archer Rd. CV8: Ken 5C **34**
Archers Spinney CV21: Hillm 3F **47**
Archery Rd. CV7: Mer 5A **10**
Arches Bus. Cen.
CV21: Rugby 4A **42**
Arches Ind. Est. CV21: Rugby 5B **42**
Arches Ind. Estate, The
CV5: Cov 1C **24**
Arches La. CV21: Rugby 4A **42**
Arch Rd. CV2: Cov 5E **21**
Arden Cl. CV7: Mer 5A **10**
CV22: Bil 6D **44**
Arden Ct. CV3: Bin W 2B **36**
Arden Rd. CV8: Ken 5F **35**
CV12: Bulk 4E **9**
Arden St. CV5: Cov 3B **24**
Arena Health & Fitness Club *5G **13***
(off Ricoh Arena)
Arena, The (Ice Rink) 4B **4** (2D **24**)
Arena Retail Pk. CV6: Longf 5H **13**
Argent Ct. CV4: Canly 6G **23**
Argyle St. CV21: Rugby 6A **42**
(not continuous)
Argyll St. CV2: Cov 1A **26**
Ariel Way CV22: Bil 5D **44**
Arkle Dr. CV2: Walsg S 3F **21**
Arlidge Cres. CV8: Ken 4G **35**
Armfield St. CV6: Cov 1A **20**
Armorial Rd. CV3: Cov 6D **24**
Armscott Rd. CV2: Cov 4C **20**
(not continuous)
Armson Rd. CV7: Exh 6E **7**
Armstrong Av. CV3: Cov 3B **26**
Armstrong Cl. CV22: Bil 2E **45**
Arne Rd. CV2: Walsg S 4G **21**
Arnhem Cnr. CV3: W'hall 6D **26**
Arnills Way CV23: Kils 6C **48**
Arno Ho. CV3: W'hall 6B **26**
Arnold Av. CV3: Cov 1E **31**
Arnold Cl. CV22: Rugby 1G **45**
Arnold St. CV21: Rugby 6H **41**
Arnold Vs. CV21: Rugby 6H **41**
Arnside Cl. CV1: Cov 1G **5** (6G **19**)
Arthingworth Cl. CV3: Bin 3E **27**
Arthur Alford Ho. CV12: Bed 5B **6**
Arthur St. CV1: Cov 1F **5** (6F **19**)
CV8: Ken 3E **35**
Arthur Vick CV4: Canly 2G **29**
Arundel Rd. CV3: Cov 6F **25**
CV12: Bulk 3E **9**
Arundel Way CV22: Caw 3A **44**
Ascot Cl. CV3: W'hall 6C **26**
CV12: Bed 2F **7**
Ashbridge Rd. CV5: Cov 6G **17**
Ashburton Rd. CV2: Cov 2E **21**
Ashby Cl. CV3: Bin 4F **27**
Ashby Dr. NN6: Crick 4H **49**
Ashby Rd. CV23: Kils 6C **48**
Ashcombe Dr. CV4: Tile H 1D **22**
Ash Ct. CV22: Rugby 4E **45**
Ashcroft Cl. CV2: Walsg S 2G **21**
Ashcroft Way CV2: Walsg S 2H **21**
Ashdale Cl. CV3: Bin W 2C **36**
Ashdene Gdns. CV8: Ken 4F **35**
Ashdown Cl. CV3: Bin 4D **26**
Ash Dr. CV8: Ken 4E **35**
Ashfield Av. CV4: Tile H 3B **22**
Ashfield Rd. CV8: Ken 5F **35**
Ashford Dr. CV12: Bed 3E **7**
ASH GREEN 2E **13**
Ash Grn. La. CV7: Ash G 2E **13**
Ash Gro. CV7: Ash G 1E **13**
Ashington Gro. CV3: Cov 6A **26**
Ashington Rd. CV12: Bed 5A **6**
Ashlawn Railway Cutting
Nature Reserve 3A **46**
Ashlawn Rd.
CV22: Hillm, Rugby 6E **45**
Ashman Av. CV23: Long L 4B **40**
Ashmore Rd. CV6: Cov 6D **18**
Ashorne Cl. CV2: Cov 6C **14**
(not continuous)
ASHOW 6H **35**
Ashow Cl. CV8: Ken 4F **35**
Ash Priors Cl. CV4: Tile H 3F **23**
Ash Tree Av. CV4: Tile H 2E **23**
Ashurst Cl. CV6: Longf 3B **14**
Ashwood Av. CV6: Cov 5B **18**
Ashwood Ct. CV21: Rugby 5F **41**
Ashworth Cl. NN6: Crick 2H **49**
Aspen Cl. CV4: Tile H 3B **22**
Aspen Ct. CV8: Ken 4G **35**
Aspen Dr. CV6: Longf 2C **14**
Assheton Cl. CV22: Bil 3C **44**
Asthill Cft. CV3: Cov 4E **25**
Asthill Gro. CV3: Cov 4E **25**
Astley Av. CV6: Cov 6G **13**
Astley La. CV12: Bed 2A **6**
Astley Pl. CV21: Hillm 4F **47**
Aston Rd. CV5: Cov 3B **24**
Astoria Dr. CV4: Tile H 1A **22**
Athena Gdns. CV6: Cov 1A **20**
Atherston Pl. CV4: Canly 6H **23**
Athol Rd. CV2: Walsg S 4G **21**
Attoxhall Rd. CV2: Cov 6E **21**
Attwood Cres. CV2: Cov 3C **20**
Auburndale Av. CV4: Tile H 1A **22**
Augustus Rd. CV1: Cov 1H **5** (6H **19**)
Austin Dr. CV6: Cov 3A **20**
Austin Drive (Park & Ride) 3A **20**
Aventine Way CV21: Rugby 2F **41**
Avenue, The CV3: Cov 6A **26**
Avenue Rd. CV8: Ken 2B **34**
CV21: Rugby 5E **41**
Avocet Cl. CV2: Ald G 5B **14**
CV23: Brow 2G **43**
Avon Cl. CV12: Bulk 1D **8**
Avon Ct. CV21: Rugby 5G **41**
Avondale Rd. CV5: Cov 4C **24**
CV8: Bran 4D **36**
Avon Ind. Est. CV21: Rugby 4A **42**
Avonmere CV21: N'bld A 2E **41**
Avon Rd. CV4: Canly 6F **23**
CV8: Ken 5C **34**
Avon St. CV2: Cov 5B **20**
CV21: Rugby 5G **41**
CV23: Clift D 5C **42**
Avon Vw. Pk. Homes
CV8: Rytn D 4E **33**
Avon Way CV23: Long L 5B **40**
Awson St. CV6: Cov 4H **19**
Axholme Rd. CV2: Cov 6E **21**
Aylesbury Ct. *CV6: Cov 3F **19***
(off Gressingham Gro.)
Aylesdene Ct. CV5: Cov 4B **24**
Aylesford St. CV1: Cov 1H **5** (6G **19**)
Aynho Cl. CV5: E Grn 1E **23**

B

Babbacombe Rd. CV3: Cov 6F **25**
Bablake Cl. CV6: Cov 2B **18**
Back La. CV7: Mer 6A **16**
CV23: Long L 5A **40**
Bacon's Yd. CV6: Cov 6H **13**
Badby Leys CV22: Rugby 4F **45**
Badger Rd. CV3: Bin 4D **26**
Badgers Cl. CV23: Long L 5H **39**
Baffin Cl. CV22: Bil 2E **45**
BAGINTON 4H **31**
Baginton Rd. CV3: Cov 6D **24**
(not continuous)
Bagshaw Cl. CV8: Rytn D 5G **33**
Bailey Rd. CV23: Brow 2H **43**
Bailey's La. CV23: Long L 4A **40**
Bakehouse La.
CV21: Rugby 6F **41**
Baker Ho. CV22: Bil 3C **44**
Bakers La. CV5: Cov 1A **24**
Baker St. CV6: Longf 2B **14**
Bakewell Cl. CV3: Bin 4F **27**
Balcombe Ct. CV22: Hillm 3C **46**
Balcombe Rd. CV22: Hillm 3B **46**
Baldwin Cft. CV6: Cov 1B **20**
Balfour Pl. CV22: Hillm 2B **46**
Ballantine Rd. CV6: Cov 4D **18**
Ballingham Cl. CV4: Tile H 2E **23**
Balliol Rd. CV2: Cov 6B **20**
Balmoral Cl. CV2: Cov 4F **21**
Banks, The CV23: Kils 6C **48**
Bankside Cl. CV3: Cov 6H **25**
Banks Rd. CV6: Cov 5C **18**
Bank St. CV21: Rugby 6G **41**
Banner La. CV4: Tile H 6B **16**
Bantam Gro. CV6: Cov 5C **12**
Bantock Rd. CV4: Tile H 2C **22**
Baptist Cl. CV2: Ald G 4D **14**
Barbican Ri. CV2: Cov 2E **27**
Barbridge Cl. CV12: Bulk 4E **9**
Barbridge Rd. CV12: Bulk 3D **8**
Barby La. CV22: Hillm 3D **46**
CV23: Barby 3D **46**
BARBY NORTOFT 2B **48**
Barby Rd. CV22: Rugby 1G **45**
CV23: Barby, Kils 5A **48**
Bardley Dr. CV6: Cov 4E **19**
Barford Cl. CV3: Bin 5D **26**
Barford M. CV8: Ken 4F **35**
Barford Rd. CV8: Ken 5F **35**
Barker's Butts La.
CV6: Cov 1A **4** (5B **18**)
Barley Cl. CV21: Hillm 3E **47**
Barley Cft. NN6: Crick 2H **49**
Barley Lea, The CV3: Cov 4B **26**
Barlow Rd. CV2: Ald G 5D **14**
Barnack Av. CV3: Cov 1D **30**
BARNACLE 2G **15**
Barnacle La. CV12: Bulk 5E **9**
Barn Cl. CV5: Cov 5G **17**
Barnes Ct. CV1: Cov 1C **4** (6E **19**)
Barnfield Av. CV5: Alle 3E **17**
Barnstaple Cl. CV5: Alle 6D **16**
Barnwell Cl. CV22: Dunc 1C **50**
Baron Leigh Dr.
CV4: Westw H 6B **22**
Baron's Cft. CV3: Cov 5G **25**
Baron's Fld. Rd. CV3: Cov 5F **25**
Barracks Way CV1: Cov 4D **4** (2E **25**)
Barras Ct. CV2: Cov 6A **20**
Barras Grn. CV2: Cov 6A **20**
Barras Grn. Bungs. CV2: Cov 6A **20**
Barras La. CV1: Cov 3A **4** (1D **24**)
Barrie Way CV2: Cov 4A **20**
Barrington Rd. CV22: Bil 1C **44**
Bar Rd. CV3: Cov 4G **25**
Barrow Cl. CV2: Walsg S 4H **21**
Barrowfield Ct. CV8: Ken 4D **34**
Barrowfield La. CV8: Ken 4D **34**
Barrow Rd. CV8: Ken 4D **34**
Barston Cl. CV6: Cov 5A **14**
Barter Pl. CV21: Rugby 5A **42**
Bartholomew Ct. CV3: Cov 6H **25**
Bartlett Cl. CV6: Cov 6G **13**
Bartley Wlk. CV23: Long L 5B **40**
Barton Rd. CV6: Cov 6H **13**
CV12: Bed 3E **7**
CV22: Bil 3D **44**
Bartons Ct. CV2: Cov 6A **20**
Barton's Mdw. CV2: Cov 4B **20**
Baseley Way CV6: Longf 4F **13**
Basford Brook Dr. CV6: Longf 3H **13**
Basildon Wlk. CV2: Walsg S 3G **21**
Bassett Rd. CV6: Cov 5C **18**
Batemans Acre Sth. CV6: Cov 6C **18**
Bates Rd. CV5: Cov 5A **24**
Bath St. CV1: Cov 1F **5** (6F **19**)
CV21: Rugby 6H **41**
Bath St. M. CV21: Rugby 5H **41**
Bathurst Cl. CV22: Bil 3E **45**
Bathurst Rd. CV6: Cov 4C **18**
Bathway Rd. CV3: Finh 2C **30**
Batsford Rd. CV6: Cov 5B **18**
Battalion Ct. CV6: Cov 1C **18**
Bawnmore Ct. CV22: Bil 3D **44**
Bawnmore Pk. CV22: Bil 4E **45**
Bawnmore Rd. CV22: Bil 3D **44**
Baxter Cl. CV4: Tile H 2E **23**
Bayley La. CV1: Cov 4E **5** (2F **25**)
Bayliss Av. CV6: Longf 4A **14**
Bayton Ind. Est. CV7: Exh 1A **14**
Bayton Rd. CV7: Exh 1A **14**
Bayton Rd. Ind. Est. CV7: Exh 6F **7**
Bayton Way CV7: Exh 1C **14**
Baytree Cl. CV2: Cov 1D **20**
Bazzard Rd. CV11: Bram 1H **9**
Beacon Rd. CV6: Cov 5E **13**
Beaconsfield Av.
CV22: Rugby 2G **45**
Beaconsfield Rd. CV2: Cov 2B **26**
Beake Av. CV6: Cov 1D **18**
Beamish Cl. CV2: Walsg S 4G **21**
Beanfield Av. CV3: Finh 2B **30**
Bear Rock Climbing Cen. 1G **29**
Beatty Dr. CV22: Bil 1D **44**
Beauchamp Ho. CV1: Cov 5C **4**
Beauchamp Rd. CV8: Ken 6C **34**
Beaudesert Rd. CV5: Cov 3C **24**
Beaufort Dr. CV3: Bin 5F **27**
Beaumaris Cl. CV5: Alle 5D **16**
Beaumont Ct. *CV6: Cov 6C **18***
(off Beaumont Cres.)
Beaumont Cres. CV6: Cov 6C **18**
Beaumont Rd. CV7: Ker E 2B **12**
Beausale Cft. CV5: E Grn 1E **23**
Beche Way CV5: Cov 5F **17**
Beckbury Rd. CV2: Walsg S 3F **21**
Beckett Rd. CV2: Cov 4B **20**
Beckfoot Cl. CV21: Brow 1B **42**

Brookside Av.—Chetwode Cl.

Brookside Av. CV5: Cov 1G 23
CV8: Ken 4C 34
Brookside Cl. CV22: Rugby 2G 45
Brookstray Flats CV5: E Grn 1F 23
Brook St. CV8: Wols 6E 37
CV12: Bed 1F 7
Brookvale Av. CV3: Bin 3E 27
Brook Vw. CV22: Dunc 2B 50
Broom Cl. CV22: Bil 2E 45
Broome Cft. CV6: Cov 5D 12
Broomfield Pl. CV5: Cov 2C 24
(not continuous)
Broomfield Rd. CV5: Cov 3B 24
Broomybank CV8: Ken 2F 35
Browett Rd. CV6: Cov 5C 18
Browning Rd. CV2: Cov 1C 26
CV21: Hillm 3F 47
Brownshill Ct. CV6: Cov 2B 18
BROWNSHILL GREEN 1H 17
Brownshill Grn. Rd. CV5: Alle 1H 17
CV6: Cov 1H 17
Brown's La. CV5: Alle 2E 17
BROWNSOVER 2B 42
Brownsover La. CV21: Brow 2H 41
Brownsover Rd.
CV21: N'bld A, Rugby 2E 41
Bruce Rd. CV6: Cov 2C 18
CV7: Exh 1H 13
Bruce Williams Way
CV22: Rugby 1H 45
Brudenell Cl. CV22: Caw 3A 44
Brunel Cl. CV2: Cov 1H 25
Brunes Ct. CV21: Brow 2B 42
Brunswick Cl. CV21: Rugby 3A 42
Brunswick Rd.
CV1: Cov 5A 4 (2C 24)
Bruntingthorpe Way CV3: Bin 4E 27
Brunton Cl. CV3: Bin 3H 27
Bryanston Cl. CV2: Walsg S 6G 21
Bryant Rd. CV7: Exh 1A 14
CV23: Brow 2G 43
Brympton Rd. CV3: Cov 2C 26
Bryn Jones Cl. CV3: Bin 4F 27
Bryn Rd. CV6: Cov 3H 19
Bryony Cl. CV12: Bed 5C 6
Bubbenhall Rd.
CV8: Bag, Bubb 5H 31
Buccleuch Cl. CV22: Dunc 1C 50
Buchanan Cl. CV4: Tile H 1A 22
Buchanan Rd.
CV22: Bil, Rugby 2E 45
Buckfast Cl. CV3: Cov 1G 31
Buckhold Dr. CV5: Cov 5F 17
Buckingham Ri. CV5: Cov 6F 17
Buckland Rd. CV6: Cov 6D 12
Bucknill Cres. CV21: Hillm 3F 47
Bucknills La. NN6: Crick 3H 49
Buckwell La. CV23: Clift D 4E 43
Budbrooke Cl. CV2: Cov 6D 14
BULKINGTON 4E 9
Bulkington Rd. CV12: Bed 4G 7
Bullfield Av. CV4: Tile H 3C 22
Bullimore Gro. CV8: Ken 6E 35
Bull's Head La. CV3: Cov 2B 26
Bull Yd. CV1: Cov 4C 4 (2E 25)
Bulwer Rd. CV6: Cov 3C 18
Bulwick Cl. CV3: Bin 3H 27
Bunkers Hill La.
CV23: Bret, Chu L 4H 37
Burbages La. CV6: Longf 3F 13
Burbury Cl. CV12: Bed 2G 7
Burges, The CV1: Cov 2D 4 (1E 25)
Burlington Rd. CV2: Cov 6H 19
(not continuous)
Burlywood Cl. CV5: Alle 2F 17
Burnaby Rd. CV6: Cov 1D 18
Burnham Rd. CV3: Cov 6A 26
Burnsall Gro. CV5: Cov 4H 23
Burnsall Rd. CV5: Cov 4G 23
Burnsall Rd. Ind. Est.
CV5: Cov 4G 23
Burnside CV3: Bin 2G 27
CV22: Rugby 1E 45
Burns Rd. CV2: Cov 1C 26
Burns Wlk. CV12: Bed 5G 7
Burroughs Cl. CV2: Cov 4B 20
Burrow Hill Hill Fort 1G 11
Burrow Hill La. CV7: Cor 1G 11
Burton Cl. CV5: Alle 6G 11
BURTON GREEN 2A 28
Bury Dyke NN6: Crick 2H 49
Busby Cl. CV3: Bin 5F 27
Bushbery Av. CV4: Tile H 3D 22
Bush Cl. CV4: Tile H 1D 22
Bushelton Cl. CV1: Cov 6F 5 (3F 25)
Butchers La. CV5: Alle 4G 17
Butler Cl. CV8: Ken 1G 35
Butler Cres. CV7: Exh 5E 7
Butlers Leap CV21: Rugby 4A 42
Butlin Rd. CV6: Cov 4E 13
CV21: Rugby 6B 42
Buttercup Way CV12: Bed 4B 6
Butterfly Wlk. CV2: Cov 2C 20
Buttermere CV21: Brow 2B 42
Buttermere Cl. CV3: Bin 5F 27
Butterworth Dr. CV4: Westw H 6E 23
Butt La. CV5: Alle 3E 17
Butts CV1: Cov 5A 4 (2D 24)
Butts Arena, The 2C 24
Butts Rd. CV1: Cov 4A 4 (2C 24)
Byfield Rd. CV6: Cov 5A 18
Byron Av. CV12: Bed 4H 7
Byron St. CV1: Cov 1E 5 (6F 19)
Bywater Cl. CV3: Cov 2D 30

C

Cadden Dr. CV4: Tile H 2F 23
Cadet Cl. CV3: Cov 3A 26
Cadman Cl. CV12: Bed 3G 7
Caesar Rd. CV8: Ken 5C 34
Caister Hall CV1: Cov 3G 5
Caithness Cl. CV5: E Grn 6E 17
Calcott Ho. CV3: W'hall 6B 26
Caldecote Rd. CV6: Cov 5E 19
Caldecott Ct. CV21: Rugby 5H 41
Caldecott Pl. CV21: Rugby 1A 46
Caldecott St. CV21: Rugby 1A 46
Calder Cl. CV3: Cov 5G 25
CV12: Bulk 4D 8
Calgary Cl. CV3: Bin 2G 27
Calico Way CV6: Cov 3F 19
Callier Cl. CV22: Caw 3B 44
Calmere Cl. CV2: Walsg S 2F 21
Caludon Castle 5E 21
CALUDON CENTRE 4F 21
Caludon Pk. Av. CV2: Cov 5E 21
Caludon Rd. CV2: Cov 6A 20
Calverly Ct. CV3: Cov 4A 26
Calvert Cl. CV3: Cov 6F 25
CV21: Brow 2C 42
Calvestone Pl. CV22: Caw 4A 44
Calvestone Rd. CV22: Caw 4A 44
Calvestone Sq. CV22: Caw 3A 44
Cambridge St. CV1: Cov 5G 19
CV21: Rugby 6A 42
Camden St. CV2: Cov 6A 20
Camelia Rd. CV2: Cov 6B 14
Camelot Gro. CV8: Ken 3G 35
Cameron Cl. CV5: Alle 3E 17
Campbell St. CV21: Rugby 6E 41
Campion Cl. CV3: Cov 6F 25
CV12: Bed 4B 6
Campion Way CV23: Brow 1B 42
Campling Cl. CV12: Bulk 4D 8
Camville CV3: Bin 2G 27
Canal Ho. CV1: Cov 1D 4 (6E 19)
Canal Rd. CV6: Cov 2H 19
Canalside CV6: Longf 2B 14
Canberra Ct. CV12: Bed 4D 6
Canberra Rd. CV2: Ald G 4C 14
Canford Cl. CV3: Finh 3E 31
CANLEY 6G 23
Canley Ford CV5: Cov 5A 24
(not continuous)
Canley Garden
Cemetery & Crematorium
CV4: Canly 6H 23
Canley Rd. CV5: Cov 5H 23
(not continuous)
Canley Station (Rail) 3H 23
Canley Woodlands
Local Nature Reserve 5C 22
Cannas Ct. CV4: Canly 6H 23
Cannocks La. CV4: Canly 6H 23
Cannon Cl. CV4: Cov 6A 24
Cannon Hill Rd. CV4: Canly 6H 23
Cannon Pk. Rd. CV4: Canly 1A 30
Cannon Pk. Shop. Cen.
CV4: Canly 6G 23
Canon Dr. CV7: Ash G 2F 13
Canon Hudson Cl. CV3: W'hall 6C 26
Canterbury Cl. CV8: Ken 5G 35
Canterbury St.
CV1: Cov 1G 5 (6G 19)
Cantlow Cl. CV5: E Grn 1E 23
Capmartin Rd. CV6: Cov 3D 18
Capulet Cl. CV3: W'hall 6C 26
CV22: Bil 5E 45
Carabiners, The CV3: Cov 3A 26
Caradoc Cl. CV2: Cov 3D 20
Cardale Cft. CV3: Bin 3F 27
Cardiff Cl. CV3: W'hall 1D 32
Cardigan Rd. CV12: Bed 5A 6
Carding Cl. CV5: E Grn 6D 16
Carew Wlk. CV22: Bil 2C 44
Carey St. CV6: Cov 1B 20
Cargill Cl. CV6: Longf 3H 13
Carlton Cl. CV12: Bulk 3D 8
Carlton Ct. CV5: Cov 1B 24
CV23: Clift D 4D 42
Carlton Gdns. CV5: Cov 4C 24
Carlton Rd. CV6: Cov 1H 19
CV22: Bil 2D 44
Carmelite Rd.
CV1: Cov 4H 5 (2G 25)
Carnbroe Av. CV3: Bin 5F 27
Carnegie Cl. CV3: W'hall 1B 32
Caroline Pl. CV12: Bulk 4E 9
Carolyn La. Ct. *CV21: Rugby 5F 41*
(off Blackman Way)
Carpenter Rd. CV2: Cov 4B 20
Carrick Hall CV1: Cov 3F 5
Carroll Cres. CV2: Cov 4A 20
Carsal Cl. CV7: Ash G 3F 13
Carter Rd. CV3: Cov 4A 26
Carthusian Rd. CV3: Cov 4E 25
Cartmel Cl. CV5: E Grn 6E 17
Carvell Cl. CV5: Alle 1F 17
Carver Cl. CV2: Cov 2E 27
Cascade Cl. CV3: Cov 6G 25
Cashmore Rd. CV8: Ken 4G 35
CV12: Bed 5C 6
Cash's Bus. Cen. CV1: Cov 5F 19
Cash's La. CV1: Cov 4F 19
Casita Gro. CV8: Ken 4G 35
Caspian Way CV2: Walsg S 2G 21
Cassandra Cl. CV4: Canly 3H 29
Castle Cl. CV3: Cov 6F 25
Castle Combe CV21: Rugby 3H 41
Castle Ct. CV8: Ken 2E 35
CASTLE END 5E 35
Castle Farm Recreation Cen. 4C 34
CASTLE GREEN 3B 34
Castle Grn. CV8: Ken 3B 34
Castle Gro. CV8: Ken 4C 34
Castle Hill CV8: Ken 3C 34
Castle M. CV21: Rugby 6H 41
Castle Mound Way
CV23: Brow 1H 43
Castle Pl. Ind. Est. CV1: Cov 1F 5
Castle Rd. CV8: Ken 3C 34
Castle St. CV1: Cov 1G 5
CV21: Rugby 6H 41
Castle Yd. CV1: Cov 4E 5
Catesby Rd. CV6: Cov 2D 18
CV22: Rugby 2B 46
Cathedral Lanes Shop. Cen.
CV1: Cov 3D 4 (1E 25)
Catherine St. CV2: Cov 2H 5 (1H 25)
Catherine Ward Hall *CV12: Bed 1F 7*
(off Mill Ter.)
Cathiron La.
CV23: Harb M, Lit L 1A 40
Cavans Cl. CV3: Bin 4G 27
Cavans Way CV3: Bin 4G 27
Cave Cl. CV22: Caw 3A 44
Cavell Ct. CV21: Rugby 6B 42
Cavendish Cl. CV22: Caw 2A 44
Cavendish Rd. CV4: Tile H 2C 22
Cawnpore Rd. CV6: Cov 6D 12
CAWSTON 4A 44
Cawston Grange Dr.
CV22: Caw 3A 44
Cawston La. CV22: Caw, Dunc 4A 44
Cawston Way CV22: Bil 3C 44
Cawthorne Cl.
CV1: Cov 1H 5 (6G 19)
Cecily Rd. CV3: Cov 5F 25
Cedar Av. CV8: Rytn D 5H 33
Cedar Ct. CV5: Alle 4E 17
Cedars, The CV7: Exh 6E 7
Cedars Av. CV6: Cov 5A 18
Cedars Rd. CV7: Exh 5F 7
Cedric Cl. CV3: W'hall 1C 32
Celandine CV23: Brow 1C 42
Celandine Rd. CV2: Cov 6D 14
Celandine Way CV12: Bed 4C 6
Celilo Wlk. CV6: Ker E 4C 12
Celtic Way NN6: Crick 2D 48
Centaur Rd. CV5: Cov 2B 24
Centenary Rd. CV4: Canly 5H 23
Central Av. CV2: Cov 2A 26
Central Blvd.
CV6: Ash G, Ker E 2B 12
CV7: Ash G 2B 12
CV7: Ker E 3B 12
Central Bldgs. CV3: Cov 6C 4
Central City Ind. Est.
CV6: Cov 5H 19
Central Pk. Dr. CV23: Brow 1G 43
Central Six Retail Pk.
CV3: Cov 6B 4 (3D 24)
Chace Av. CV3: W'hall 1B 32
Chaceley Cl. CV2: Walsg S 2G 21
Chadwick Cl. CV5: E Grn 1F 23
Chalfont Cl. CV5: Cov 6F 17
CV12: Bed 2E 7
Challenge Bus. Pk. CV1: Cov 5F 19
Challenge Cl. CV1: Cov 6F 19
Chaloner Cl. CV2: Cov 6B 14
Chamberlaine St. CV12: Bed 3F 7
Chamberlain Rd. CV21: Hillm 3F 47
Chamberlains Grn. CV6: Cov 3B 18
Chancellors Cl. CV4: Canly 2H 29
Chandler Ct. CV5: Cov 4D 24
Chandos St. CV2: Cov 1A 26
Channel Way CV6: Longf 2B 14
Chantries, The CV1: Cov 5G 19
Chapel Farm Cl. CV3: W'hall 6C 26
CHAPEL FIELDS 2B 24
CHAPEL GREEN 1A 10
Chapel La. CV7: Barn 2H 15
CV8: Rytn D 4G 33
NN6: Crick 3H 49
Chapelry La. CV23: Long L 5B 40
Chapel St. CV1: Cov 2C 4 (1E 25)
CV12: Bed 3F 7
(not continuous)
CV21: Rugby 6G 41
CV23: Kils 6C 48
CV23: Long L 5A 40
Chard Rd. CV3: Bin 4D 26
Chariot Way CV21: Rugby 2G 41
Charity Rd. CV7: Ker E 1C 12
Charlecote Rd. CV6: Cov 6C 12
Charles Eaton Ct. CV12: Bed 3C 6
Charles Eaton Rd. CV12: Bed 3D 6
Charlesfield Rd. CV22: Rugby 3G 45
Charles St. CV1: Cov 1G 5 (6G 19)
CV21: Rugby 6F 41
Charles Warren Cl.
CV21: Rugby 6H 41
Charlewood Rd. CV6: Cov 6D 12
Charlotte St. CV21: Rugby 6H 41
Charminster Dr. CV3: Cov 2F 31
Charolais Cl. CV21: Rugby 5A 42
Charter Av. CV4: Canly 5F 23
CV4: Tile H 5B 22
Charterhouse Rd.
CV1: Cov 5H 5 (2G 25)
Charter Rd. CV22: Hillm 3C 46
Charwelton Dr. CV21: Brow 3C 42
Chase La. CV8: Ken 1A 34
Chatham Cl. CV3: Cov 4C 26
Chatsworth Gro. CV8: Ken 3G 35
Chatsworth Ri. CV3: Cov 1G 31
Chaucer Rd. CV22: Rugby 5F 45
Chauntry Pl. CV1: Cov 2E 5 (1F 25)
Cheadle Cl. CV2: Ald G 4A 14
Cheam Cl. CV6: Cov 1A 20
Cheetah Rd. CV1: Cov 6F 5 (3F 25)
Chelmarsh CV6: Cov 4E 19
Chelney Wlk. CV3: Bin 3G 27
Chelsey Rd. CV2: Cov 2E 21
Cheltenham Cl. CV12: Bed 2F 7
Cheltenham Cft. CV2: Walsg S 3F 21
Chelveston Rd. CV6: Cov 5A 18
Chelwood Gro. CV2: Walsg S 2F 21
Chenies Cl. CV5: Cov 1F 23
Chepstow Cl. CV3: W'hall 1C 32
Chequer St. CV12: Bulk 4E 9
Cheriton Cl. CV5: Cov 6H 17
Cherrybrook Way CV2: Cov 1C 20
Cherryburn Wlk. *CV22: Bil 1E 45*
(off Stourhead Rd.)
Cherry Cl. CV6: Cov 6F 13
Cherry Gro. CV22: Bil 3E 45
Cherry Orchard CV8: Ken 3E 35
Cherry Way CV8: Ken 3E 35
Cherrywood Gro. CV5: Alle 5D 16
Cherwell Way CV23: Long L 5B 40
Chesford Cres. CV6: Cov 6B 14
Cheshire Cl. CV3: Cov 3A 26
CV22: Bil 3C 44
Chesholme Rd. CV6: Cov 5D 12
Chesils, The CV3: Cov 1E 31
Chester St. CV1: Cov 2A 4 (1D 24)
CV21: Rugby 5A 42
Chesterton Rd. CV6: Cov 3C 18
Chestnut Av. CV8: Ken 5D 34
Chestnut Fld. CV21: Rugby 6G 41
Chestnut Gro. CV4: Tile H 2E 23
CV8: Wols 6E 37
Chestnut Rd. CV12: Bed 2H 7
Chestnuts, The CV3: Cov 4A 26
CV12: Bed 4C 6
Chestnut Tree Av. CV4: Tile H 2E 23
Cheswick Cl. CV6: Cov 3A 20
Chetton Av. CV6: Cov 5E 19
Chetwode Cl. CV5: Cov 6F 17

Cheveral Av.—Crondal Rd.

Cheveral Av. CV6: Cov 4D 18
Cheveral Rd. CV12: Bed 3E 7
Cheviot, The CV4: Canly 6H 23
Cheviot Wlk. CV23: Long L 5A 40
CHEYLESMORE 4F 25
Cheylesmore CV1: Cov 5D 4 (2E 25)
Cheylesmore Shop. Pde.
CV3: Cov 5F 25
Chicory Dr. CV23: Brow 1B 42
Chideock Hill CV3: Cov 6C 24
Chiel Cl. CV5: E Grn 6D 16
Chillaton Rd. CV6: Cov 6D 12
Chiltern Ct. CV6: Cov 5C 18
Chiltern Leys CV6: Cov 6C 18
Chilterns, The CV5: Cov 6F 17
Chingford Rd. CV6: Longf 4A 14
Chorley Way CV6: Cov 4E 19
Christchurch Rd. CV6: Cov 4B 18
Christopher Hooke Ho.
CV6: Cov 1G 19
Chudleigh Rd. CV2: Cov 3E 21
Church Cl. CV8: Rytn D 4G 33
Church Ct. CV6: Cov 1B 18
Church Dr. CV8: Ken 3D 34
CHURCH END 1B 26
Churchill Av. CV6: Cov 1F 19
CV8: Ken 2E 35
Churchill Rd. CV22: Rugby 2G 45
Church La. CV2: Cov 1B 26
CV5: E Grn 5A 16
CV7: Ash G 1G 13
CV7: Cor 1D 10
CV23: Thurl 6A 50
CHURCH LAWFORD 4E 39
Church Lawford Bus. Cen.
CV23: Chu L 4C 38
Church Pk. Cl. CV6: Cov 1B 18
Church Rd. CV8: Bag 4G 31
CV8: Rytn D 4H 33
CV23: Chu L 4E 39
Churchside Arc. *CV21: Rugby 6G 41*
(off Lit. Church St.)
Church St. CV1: Cov 6F 19
CV12: Bulk 4E 9
CV21: Rugby 6G 41
CV23: Clift D 4E 43
NN6: Crick 2H 49
Church Vw. CV8: Rytn D 4G 33
Church Wlk. CV5: Alle 4G 17
CV12: Bed 4F 7
CV21: Rugby 6H 41
CV22: Bil 3D 44
CV23: Kils 5C 48
CV23: Thurl 5A 50
Church Way CV12: Bed 4F 7
Chylds Ct. CV5: Cov 5E 17
Cineworld Cinema
Rugby 3H 41
City Arc. CV1: Cov 4C 4 (2E 25)
Clara St. CV2: Cov 2A 26
Clare Ct. CV21: Rugby 6F 41
Claremont Cl. CV12: Bulk 2D 8
Claremont Rd. CV21: Rugby 6A 42
Claremont Wlk. CV5: Alle 4G 17
Clarence Rd. CV21: Rugby 6E 41
Clarence St. CV1: Cov 1H 5 (6G 19)
Clarendon M. CV5: Cov 3B 24
Clarendon Rd. CV8: Ken 5E 35
Clarendon St. CV5: Cov 3B 24
Clarke's Av. CV8: Ken 5E 35
Clark St. CV6: Cov 1A 20
Classic Dr. CV6: Longf 5G 13
Claverdon Rd. CV5: E Grn 1F 23
Claycroft CV4: Canly 1G 29
Clay Hill La.
CV23: Lit L, Long L 3H 39
Clay La. CV2: Cov 6A 20
CV5: Alle 4C 10
Clayton Rd. CV6: Cov 5A 18
Clements Cl. CV8: Ken 3E 35
Clements St. CV2: Cov 1A 26
Clement Way CV22: Caw 3A 44
Clennon Ri. CV2: Cov 2D 20
Cleveland Rd. CV2: Cov 6A 20
CV12: Bulk 3D 8
Clifden Gro. CV8: Ken 2G 35
Clifford Bri. Rd. CV2: Walsg S 5F 21
CV3: Bin 2F 27
Clifton New Wharf
CV23: Clift D 4C 42
Clifton Rd. CV21: Rugby 6H 41
Clifton St. CV1: Cov 1G 5 (6G 19)
Clifton Ter. CV8: Ken 2E 35
CLIFTON UPON DUNSMORE 4E 43
Clinton Av. CV8: Ken 2B 34
Clinton La. CV8: Ken 1B 34
Clinton Rd. CV6: Cov 6H 13
Clipstone Rd. CV6: Cov 4A 18
Clock Towers Shop. Cen.
CV21: Rugby 6G 41
Cloister Cft. CV2: Walsg S 4F 21
Close, The CV8: Bran 4D 36
CV8: Ken 2E 35
Cloud Grn. CV4: Canly 6H 23
Clovelly Gdns. CV2: Cov 5C 20
Clovelly Rd. CV2: Cov 5B 20
Clover Cl. CV23: Brow 1B 42
Cloverdale Cl. CV6: Cov 4D 12
Clover Way CV12: Bed 4B 6
Clyde Rd. CV12: Bulk 3C 8
COALPIT FIELD 4H 7
Coalpit Flds. Rd. CV12: Bed 4G 7
Coalpit La. CV8: Wols 5G 37
Coat of Arms Bri. Rd.
CV3: Cov 6B 24
Cobalt Centre, The
CV3: W'hall 5C 32
Cobb Cl. CV2: Cov 6H 19
Cobbs Rd. CV8: Ken 2B 34
Cobden St. CV6: Cov 5G 19
Cockerills Mdw. CV21: Hillm 3E 47
Cock Robin Wood Nature Reserve
5E 45
Cofa Ct. CV1: Cov 5D 4
Colchester St.
CV1: Cov 2G 5 (1G 25)
Coldstream Ct. CV3: Cov 4A 26
Coldwells Ct. *CV22: Rugby 1G 45*
(off Union St.)
Colebrook Cl. CV3: Bin 2F 27
Coleby Cl. CV4: Westw H 5B 22
Cole Ct. CV6: Cov 1A 4 (6C 18)
Coleman Cl. NN6: Crick 2H 49
Coleman St. CV4: Tile H 1D 22
Coleridge Rd. CV2: Cov 1C 26
Colina Cl. CV3: W'hall 1C 32
Colledge Rd. CV6: Cov 1F 19
Collett Wlk. CV1: Cov 1A 4 (1D 24)
CV8: Ken 4D 34
Colliery La. CV7: Exh 5F 7
Colliery La. Nth. CV7: Exh 5F 7
Collingwood Av. CV22: Bil 2D 44
Collingwood Rd. CV5: Cov 2C 24
Collins Gro. CV4: Canly 1H 29
COLLYCROFT 2F 7
Colonnade Point CV6: Ker E 3B 12
Columbia Gdns. CV12: Bed 4H 7
Columbine Way CV12: Bed 5C 6
Colyere Cl. CV7: Ker E 2C 12
Comberton Cl. CV3: Bin 2G 27
Combined Court Cen.
Coventry 5E 5 (2F 25)
COMMON, THE
CV7 1C 10
CV8 1G 35
Common La. CV7: Cor 1C 10
CV8: Ken 1F 35
Common La. Ind. Est.
CV8: Ken 1G 35
Common Way CV2: Cov 4A 20
Compass Ct. CV1: Cov 3A 4 (1D 24)
Compton Ct. CV22: Dunc 5B 44
Compton Rd. CV6: Cov 6F 13
Comrie Cl. CV2: Cov 4F 21
Coney La. CV6: Longf 2C 14
Congleton Cl. CV6: Cov 6G 13
Congreve Wlk. CV12: Bed 4F 7
Conifer Cl. CV12: Bed 2G 7
Conifer Ct. CV12: Bed 2G 7
Conifer Paddock CV3: Bin 3E 27
Conifers, The CV8: Ken 5F 35
Conisbrough Keep
CV1: Cov 3G 5 (1F 25)
Coniston Cl. CV12: Bulk 3E 9
CV21: Brow 3B 42
Coniston Dr. CV5: E Grn 6B 16
Coniston Grange CV8: Ken 3E 35
Coniston Rd. CV5: Cov 3B 24
Conrad Cl. CV22: Rugby 5F 45
Conrad Rd. CV6: Cov 3C 18
Constable Cl. CV12: Bed 1E 7
Constable Rd. CV21: Hillm 2F 47
Constance Cl. CV12: Bed 6D 6
Consul Rd. CV21: Rugby 2F 41
Convent Cl. CV8: Ken 1E 35
Conway Av. CV4: Tile H 4B 22
Conway Ct. CV1: Cov 6E 5 (3F 25)
Cook Cl. CV21: Brow 2A 42
Cooke Cl. CV6: Longf 4A 14
Cook St. CV1: Cov 2D 4 (1E 25)
Coombe Av. CV3: Bin 5F 27
Coombe Country Pk. 1H 27
Coombe Ct. CV3: Bin 2G 27
Coombe Dr. CV3: Bin W 2C 36
Coombe Pk. Rd. CV3: Bin 2F 27
Coombe St. CV3: Cov 2B 26
Co-operative St. CV2: Ald G 5B 14
Coopers Mdw. CV7: Ker E 2B 12
Cope Arnolds Cl. CV6: Longf 4H 13
Copeland CV21: Brow 2A 42
Cope St. CV1: Cov 3F 5 (1F 25)
Copland Pl. CV4: Tile H 3C 22
Copperas St. CV2: Cov 6B 14
Copper Beech Cl. CV6: Cov 1G 19
Copperfield Rd. CV2: Cov 1B 26
Coppice, The CV3: Cov 4B 26
Coppice Cl. CV8: Rytn D 6H 33
Copse, The CV7: Exh 6E 7
Copse Dr. CV5: Alle 2A 16
Copsewood Grange Golf Course
3D 26
Copsewood Ter. CV3: Cov 2C 26
Copthall Ter. CV1: Cov 6C 4 (3E 25)
Copthorne Rd. CV6: Cov 2B 18
Copt Oak Cl. CV4: Westw H 6A 22
Coral Cl. CV5: Cov 2G 23
Corbet Rd. CV6: Cov 3E 19
Corbett St. CV21: Rugby 5A 42
Corbridge Pl. CV22: Caw 2A 44
Cordelia Way CV22: Bil 5E 45
Corfe Cl. CV2: Walsg S 5F 21
Corinthian Pl. CV2: Cov 4D 20
CORLEY 1G 11
CORLEY MOOR 2C 10
Corley Vw. CV7: Ash G 1E 13
Cornelius St. CV3: Cov 4F 25
Cornerstone Ho. CV1: Cov 1F 5
Cornfield, The CV3: Cov 3C 26
Cornflower Dr. CV23: Brow 1B 42
Cornhill Gro. CV8: Ken 3G 35
Cornmarket Wlk.
CV21: Rugby 5H 41
(off Craven Rd.)
Corn Mdws. CV12: Bed 4G 7
Cornwallis Rd. CV22: Bil 2B 44
Cornwall Rd. CV1: Cov 6G 5 (3G 25)
Coronation Rd.
CV1: Cov 1H 5 (6H 19)
CV23: Chu L 6D 38
Coronel Av. CV6: Longf 4G 13
Corporation St.
CV1: Cov 4C 4 (2E 25)
CV21: Rugby 6G 41
Corrie Ho. CV1: Cov 4A 4
Cosford La.
CV21: Cosf, Rugby 1G 41
(not continuous)
Cossington Rd. CV6: Cov 6G 13
Cotman Cl. CV12: Bed 2E 7
Coton Pk. Dr. CV23: Brow 1A 42
Coton Rd. CV21: Hillm 3E 47
Cotswold Dr. CV3: Finh 3E 31
Cottage Farm Lodge CV6: Cov 1C 18
Cottage Farm Rd. CV6: Cov 1C 18
Cottage Leap CV21: Rugby 5B 42
Cotterell Rd. CV21: N'bld A 3F 41
Cottesbrook Cl. CV3: Bin 3E 27
Cotton Dr. CV8: Ken 2G 35
Cotton Way CV6: Cov 3F 19
COUNDON 4B 18
Coundon Grn. CV6: Cov 3A 18
Coundon Ho. Dr. CV6: Cov 5A 18
Coundon Rd. CV1: Cov 1A 4 (6D 18)
Coundon St. CV1: Cov 2A 4 (6D 18)
Coundon Wedge Dr. CV5: Alle 1H 17
Countess Croft, The
CV3: Cov 5F 25
Country Inn M. CV23: Long L 4A 40
Courtaulds Ind. Est. CV6: Cov 4F 19
Courtaulds Way CV6: Cov 4F 19
Courthouse Cft. CV8: Ken 4G 35
COURT HOUSE GREEN 2A 20
Courtland Av. CV6: Cov 5B 18
Court Leet CV3: Bin W 2B 36
Courtleet Rd. CV3: Cov 5G 25
Courtyard, The CV8: Ken 4G 35
COVENTRY 3C 4 (1E 25)
Coventry Airpark CV3: W'hall 5B 32
COVENTRY AIRPORT 4B 32
Coventry Bees Speedway 2D 36
Coventry Bus. Pk. CV4: Cov 3H 23
CV5: Cov 3G 23
(not continuous)
Coventry Canal Basin CV1: Cov 1D 4
Coventry Cathedral 3E 5 (1F 25)
Coventry City FC 4G 13
Coventry Eastern By-Pass
CV2: Walsg S 5H 21
CV3: Bin, Bin W, W'hall 1G 27
Coventry Golf Course 4F 31
Coventry Hearsall Golf Course
4B 24
Coventry Innovation Village
CV1: Cov 6F 5 (3F 25)
Coventry Karting 1B 14
COVENTRY MYTON HOSPICE 5F 21
Coventry Point
CV1: Cov 4C 4 (2E 25)
Coventry Rd. CV2: Ald G 1F 15
CV8: Bag 3G 31
CV8: Ken 2D 34
CV8: S'lgh 6E 31
CV10: Griff, Nun 1F 7
CV12: Bed 5F 7
CV12: Bulk 1F 15
CV22: Caw 4A 44
CV22: Dunc 4A 50
CV23: Chu L 3A 38
CV23: Dunc, Thurl 4A 50
CV23: Long L 5E 39
Coventry Rd. Exhall CV7: Exh 1A 14
Coventry RUFC 2C 24
Coventry Sports & Leisure Cen.
3E 5 (1F 25)
Coventry Stadium 2D 36
Coventry Station (Rail) 6C 4 (3E 25)
Coventry St. CV2: Cov 6A 20
Coventry Trad. Est.
CV3: W'hall 3C 32
Coventry Transport Mus.
2D 4 (1E 25)
Coventry University
Alma Building 3G 5 (1G 25)
Cox St. 4F 5 (2F 25)
Gosford St. 4G 5 (2G 25)
Gulson Rd. 4G 5 (2G 25)
Priory St. 3E 5 (1F 25)
Whitefriars St. 4F 5 (2F 25)
Coventry University Techology Pk.
CV1: Cov 6F 5 (3F 25)
Coventry Watchmaker's Mus. 3B 4
Cove Pl. CV2: Cov 3C 20
Coverley Pl. CV22: Rugby 6E 41
Cowan Cl. CV22: Bil 2C 44
Cowley Rd. CV2: Cov 6D 20
Cowley Way CV23: Kils 6B 48
Cox Cres. CV22: Dunc 1C 50
Cox St. CV1: Cov 4F 5 (2F 25)
(Gosford St.)
CV1: Cov 2F 5 (1F 25)
(White St.)
Cozens Cl. CV12: Bed 2E 7
Crabmill La. CV6: Cov 3H 19
CRACKLEY 1F 35
Crackley Cotts. CV8: Ken 6F 29
Crackley Cres. CV8: Ken 6F 29
Crackley Hill CV8: Ken 1F 35
Crackley La. CV8: Ken 2B 28
Crackthorne Dr. CV23: Brow 2H 43
Craigends Av. CV3: Bin 6F 27
Crakston Cl. CV2: Cov 2E 27
Crampers Fld. CV6: Cov 5C 18
Cranborne Chase
CV2: Walsg S 5F 21
Craner's Rd. CV1: Cov 6H 19
Cranford Rd. CV5: Cov 6H 17
Crathie Cl. CV2: Cov 4F 21
Craven Av. CV3: Bin W 2A 36
Craven Rd. CV21: Rugby 5H 41
Craven St. CV5: Cov 2B 24
Crayfish Cl. CV2: Cov 2C 20
Crecy Rd. CV3: Cov 5G 25
Crediton Cl. CV3: Cov 1G 31
Crescent, The CV7: Ker E 2B 12
CV22: Caw 3B 44
Crescent Av. CV3: Cov 2C 26
Cressage Rd. CV2: Walsg S 4G 21
Creswell Pl. CV22: Caw 2A 44
Crew La. CV8: Ken 2G 35
CRICK 3H 49
Cricket Cl. CV5: Cov 1B 24
Crick Motorway Est.
NN6: Crick 2F 49
Crick Rd. CV21: Hillm 3F 47
CV23: Hillm 1A 48
Critchley Dr. CV22: Dunc 2D 50
Croft, The CV6: Longf 4H 13
CV7: Mer 5A 10
CV12: Bulk 4D 8
Croft Av. CV21: Rugby 3H 41
Croft Flds. CV12: Bed 4F 7
Croft Pool CV12: Bed 4D 6
Croft Rd. CV1: Cov 4B 4 (2D 24)
CV12: Bed 4D 6
Cromarty Cl. CV5: E Grn 6E 17
Cromes Wood CV4: Tile H 3B 22
Cromwell La.
CV4: Tile H, Westw H 2A 28
CV8: Burt G 2A 28
Cromwell Rd. CV22: Rugby 2A 46
Cromwell St. CV6: Cov 4H 19
Crondal Rd. CV7: Exh 6F 7

A-Z Coventry 55

Croome Cl.—Ellesmere Rd.

Croome Cl. CV6: Cov 6B 18
Crosbie Rd. CV5: Cov 1A 24
Cross Cheaping
CV1: Cov 3D 4 (1E 25)
(not continuous)
Crossley Ct. CV6: Cov 3H 19
Cross Point Bus. Pk.
CV2: Walsg S 2H 21
(not continuous)
Cross Rd. CV6: Cov 2G 19
CV7: Ker E 2B 12
Cross Rd. Ind. Est. CV6: Cov 3H 19
Cross St. CV21: Rugby 5A 42
CV23: Long L 4A 40
Crossway Rd. CV3: Finh 2D 30
Crowmere Rd.
CV2: Walsg S 3F 21
Crown Grn. CV6: Cov 6G 13
Crowsfurlong CV23: Brow 2H 43
Crowthorns CV21: Brow 2A 42
Croxhall St. CV12: Bed 4G 7
Croydon Cl. CV3: Cov 6G 25
Crummock Cl. CV6: Cov 5F 13
Cryfield Grange Rd.
CV4: Canly 4F 29
CV8: Canly, Ken 4F 29
Cryfield Halls CV4: Canly 2F 29
Cryfield Hgts. CV4: Canly 4G 29
Cryfield Hurst Flats
CV4: Canly 2F 29
Cryfield Redfern Flats
CV4: Canly 2F 29
Cubbington Rd. CV6: Cov 6A 14
Cuckoo La. CV1: Cov 3E 5 (1F 25)
Culworth Cl. CV21: Brow 2C 42
Culworth Ct. CV6: Cov 3G 19
Culworth Row CV6: Cov 2G 19
Cumbernauld Wlk.
CV2: Walsg S 4G 21
Cumbria Cl. CV1: Cov 1C 24
Cunningham Way CV22: Bil 1C 44
Curie Cl. CV21: Rugby 6B 42
Curlew Cl. CV2: Ald G 5B 14
Curriers Cl. CV4: Tile H 5B 22
Curriers Cl. Ind. Est.
CV4: Tile H 4B 22
Curtis Rd. CV2: Cov 4D 20
Curzon Av. CV6: Cov 2G 19
Cut-Throat La. CV23: Wool 5D 50
Cyan Pk. CV2: Cov 5A 20
Cymbeline Way CV22: Bil 5D 44
Cypress Cft. CV3: Bin 4F 27

D

Daffern Rd. CV7: Exh 5E 7
Daffodil Dr. CV12: Bed 4B 6
Daimler Rd. CV6: Cov 5E 19
Daintree Cft. CV3: Cov 5E 25
Daisy Cft. CV12: Bed 4B 6
Dalby Cl. CV3: Bin 4E 27
Dalehouse La.
CV8: Ken 2F 35 & 6A 30
Dalehouse La. Ind. Est.
CV8: Ken 2G 35
Dale St. CV21: Rugby 5G 41
Daleway Rd. CV3: Finh 3D 30
Dalkeith Av. CV22: Bil 4D 44
Dallington Rd. CV6: Cov 4A 18
Dalmeny Rd. CV4: Tile H 5B 22
Dalton Cl. CV23: Chu L 3D 38
Dalton Gdns. CV2: Cov 6F 21
Dalton Rd. CV5: Cov 4D 24
CV12: Bed 5D 6
Dalwood Way CV6: Ald G 4B 14
Dame Agnes Gro. CV6: Cov 2B 20
Dane Rd. CV2: Cov 6A 20
Danes Way NN6: Crick 1E 49
Daneswood Rd.
CV3: Bin W 2C 36
Daphne Cl. CV2: Cov 5C 14
Dark La. CV1: Cov 6E 19
CV12: Bed 5B 6
Darlaston Row CV7: Mer 5A 10
Darnford Cl. CV2: Walsg S 3F 21
Darrach Cl. CV2: Walsg S 1E 21
Dartmouth Rd. CV2: Cov 5C 20
Darwin Cl. CV2: Walsg S 4G 21
Darwin Ct. CV12: Bed 4D 6
Datchet Cl. CV5: Cov 6G 17
D'Aubeny Rd. CV4: Canly 5G 23
Davenport Rd. CV5: Cov 4D 24
Daventry Intl. Rail Freight Terminal
NN6: Crick 1D 48
(Danes Way)
NN6: Crick 2D 48
(Railport App.)
Daventry Rd. CV3: Cov 5E 25
CV22: Dunc 2D 50
CV23: Kils 6C 48
David Rd. CV1: Cov 5H 5 (2G 25)
CV7: Exh 6D 6
CV22: Bil 3D 44
Davies Rd. CV7: Exh 6D 6
Davy Ct. CV23: Brow 1G 43
Dawes Cl. CV2: Cov 6A 20
Dawley Wlk. CV2: Walsg S 3G 21
Dawlish Dr. CV3: Cov 1F 31
Dawson Rd. CV3: Cov 3B 26
Days Cl. CV1: Cov 2H 5 (1G 25)
Day's La. CV1: Cov 2H 5 (1G 25)
Deacon Cl. CV22: Rugby 2A 46
Deane Pde. CV21: Hillm 3E 47
Deane Rd. CV21: Hillm 3E 47
Deanston Cft. CV2: Walsg S 1F 21
Dean St. CV2: Cov 1A 26
Deans Way CV7: Ash G 2F 13
Deasy Ho. CV3: W'hall 1B 32
Deasy Rd. CV1: Cov 6F 5 (3F 25)
De-Compton Cl. CV7: Ker E 1C 12
Deedmore Rd.
CV2: Cov, Walsg S 2C 20
Deegan Cl. CV2: Cov 5A 20
Deepmore Rd. CV22: Bil 3D 44
Deerdale Ter. CV3: Bin 4F 27
Deerdale Way CV3: Bin 4F 27
Deerhurst M. CV22: Dunc 2C 50
Deerhurst Rd. CV6: Cov 6D 12
Deerings Rd. CV21: Hillm 3D 46
Deer Leap, The CV8: Ken 2F 35
Deighton Gro. CV3: W'hall 6C 26
Delage Cl. CV6: Ald G 4B 14
Delamere Rd. CV12: Bed 4D 6
Delaware Rd. CV3: Cov 1E 31
Delhi Av. CV6: Cov 1F 19
Delius St. CV4: Tile H 1C 22
Dell Cl. CV3: W'hall 1C 32
De Montfort Rd. CV8: Ken 2C 34
De Montfort Way
CV4: Canly 6G 23
Dempster Rd. CV12: Bed 2E 7
Denbigh Rd. CV6: Cov 4A 18
Dencer Dr. CV8: Ken 3G 35
Denemoor Ct. CV8: Ken 3F 35
Denewood Way CV8: Ken 2G 35
(not continuous)
Denham Av. CV5: Cov 6F 17
Dennis Rd. CV2: Cov 5B 20
Denshaw Cft. CV2: Walsg S 2G 21
Denton Cl. CV8: Ken 2B 34
Dering Cl. CV2: Cov 2C 20
Deronda Cl. CV12: Bed 3E 7
Derry, The NN6: Crick 3H 49
Derry Cl. CV8: Wols 5E 37
Dersingham Dr. CV6: Cov 6B 14
Derwent Cl. CV5: E Grn 6C 16
CV21: Brow 3A 42
Derwent Rd. CV6: Cov 6C 12
CV12: Bed 4E 7
Despard Rd. CV5: E Grn 5B 16
Devereux Cl. CV4: Tile H 3A 22
Devon Gro. CV2: Cov 4B 20
Devon Ox Rd. CV23: Kils 6B 48
Devonshire Cl. CV22: Caw 2B 44
Devoran Cl. CV7: Exh 6F 7
Dewar Gro. CV21: Hillm 1C 46
Dew Cl. CV22: Dunc 2C 50
Dewis Ho. CV2: Cov 1B 20
Dewsbury Av. CV3: Cov 1D 30
Dialhouse La. CV5: E Grn 6D 16
Diana Dr. CV2: Walsg S 1E 21
Dickens Rd. CV6: Cov 1C 18
CV22: Rugby 5F 45
Dickinson Ct. CV22: Rugby 2G 45
Didsbury Rd. CV7: Exh 5E 7
Digbey Cl. CV5: Alle 4F 17
Digby Pl. CV7: Mer 5A 10
Dilcock Way CV4: Tile H 5D 22
Dillam Cl. CV6: Longf 4A 14
Dillotford Av. CV3: Cov 5E 25
Dingle Cl. CV6: Cov 4C 18
Dingley Rd. CV12: Bulk 4D 8
Discovery Way CV3: Bin 5G 27
Ditton Cl. CV22: Bil 2C 44
Dodgson Cl. CV6: Longf 4A 14
Doe Bank La.
CV1: Cov 3A 4 (1C 24)
Dogberry Cl. CV3: W'hall 6C 26
Dolomite Av. CV4: Cov 3H 23
CV5: Cov 3H 23
Doncaster Cl. CV2: Cov 3D 20
Done Cerce Cl. CV22: Dunc 2C 50
Donegal Cl. CV4: Tile H 5E 23
Donnington Av. CV6: Cov 5A 18
Donnybrook Dr. CV3: Bin 3H 27
Doone Cl. CV2: Cov 4E 21
Dorchester Way CV2: Walsg S 5F 21
Dormer Harris Av.
CV4: Tile H 3D 22
Dorney Cl. CV5: Cov 4A 24
Dorothy Powell Way
CV2: Walsg S 1F 21
Dorset Cl. CV22: Caw 2B 44
Dorset Rd. CV1: Cov 5E 19
Douglas Ho. CV1: Cov 1G 5
Douglas Rd. CV21: Rugby 3A 42
Doulton Cl. CV2: Walsg S 1E 21
Doulton Ct. CV12: Bed 5A 6
Dove Cl. CV12: Bed 2C 6
Dovecote Cl. CV6: Cov 5H 17
Dovecotes, The CV5: Cov 5F 17
Dovedale Av. CV6: Cov 6H 13
Dovedale Cl. CV21: Brow 2A 42
Dover St. CV1: Cov 3B 4 (1D 24)
Dowley Cft. CV3: Bin 3H 27
Downderry Way CV6: Cov 4A 20
Downing Cres. CV12: Bed 2G 7
Downton Cl. CV2: Walsg S 2G 21
Dowty Av. CV12: Bed 5B 6
Doyle Dr. CV6: Longf 5H 13
Dragonfly Dr. CV2: Cov 2C 20
Drake St. CV6: Cov 3F 19
Draper Cl. CV8: Ken 4G 35
Drapers Ct. CV1: Cov 1D 4 (6E 19)
DRAPER'S FIELD 1D 4 (6E 19)
Drapers Flds.
CV1: Cov 1D 4 (6E 19)
Draycott Rd. CV2: Cov 3B 20
Drayson La. NN6: Crick 2H 49
Drayton Cres. CV5: E Grn 5B 16
Drayton Leys CV22: Rugby 4G 45
Drayton Rd. CV12: Bed 4H 7
Drew Cres. CV8: Ken 4E 35
Dreyer Cl. CV22: Bil 1C 44
Drinkwater Ho. *CV1: Cov 4A 4*
(off Meadow St.)
Drive, The CV2: Cov 1D 26
CV22: Dunc 1D 50
Dronfield Rd. CV2: Cov 1B 26
Drover Cl. CV21: Rugby 5H 41
Droylsdon Pk. Rd. CV3: Finh 3D 30
Druid Rd. CV2: Cov 1B 26
Drummond Cl. CV6: Cov 3B 18
Drummond Rd. CV22: Caw 3A 44
Drury La. CV21: Rugby 6G 41
Dryden Cl. CV8: Ken 5D 34
Dryden Pl. CV22: Rugby 6E 41
Dryden Wlk. CV22: Rugby 6E 41
Duckham Ct.
CV6: Cov 1A 4 (6C 18)
Dudley Rd. CV8: Ken 6C 34
Dudley St. CV6: Cov 1A 20
Duffy Pl. CV21: Hillm 3E 47
Dugdale Rd. CV6: Cov 4D 18
Duggins La. CV4: Tile H 4A 22
CV7: Berk 4A 22
Duke Barn Fld. CV2: Cov 5A 20
Dukes Jetty CV21: Rugby 6G 41
Duke St. CV5: Cov 2B 24
CV21: Rugby 5G 41
Dulverton Av. CV5: Cov 5H 17
Dulverton Ct. CV5: Cov 6H 17
Duncan Dr. CV22: Bil 5D 44
DUNCHURCH 2C 50
Dunchurch Hall CV22: Dunc 2C 50
Dunchurch Highway
CV5: Alle, Cov 4E 17
Dunchurch Rd. CV22: Rugby 5E 45
Duncroft Av. CV6: Cov 3B 18
Dunhill Av. CV4: Tile H 1C 22
Dunkirk Pl. CV3: Bin 5F 27
Dunnerdale CV21: Brow 2B 42
Dunnose Cl. CV6: Cov 2G 19
Dunrose Cl. CV2: Cov 2E 27
Dunsmore Av. CV3: W'hall 6C 26
CV22: Hillm 3C 46
Dunsmore Heath
CV22: Dunc 2C 50
Dunster Cl. CV22: Rugby 1E 45
Dunster Pl. CV6: Cov 5F 13
Dunsville Dr. CV2: Walsg S 2F 21
Dunvegan Cl. CV3: Bin 2G 27
CV8: Ken 4G 35
Durbar Av. CV6: Cov 2F 19
Durbar Av. Ind. Est.
CV6: Cov 2F 19
Durham Cl. CV7: Ker E 4B 12
Durham Cres. CV5: Alle 3E 17
Durrell Dr. CV22: Caw 3A 44
Dutton Rd. CV2: Ald G 5D 14
Dyer's La. CV8: Wols 6E 37
Dymond Rd. CV6: Cov 5E 13
Dysart Cl. CV1: Cov 1G 5 (6G 19)
Dyson Cl. CV21: Hillm 2D 46
Dyson St. CV4: Tile H 1C 22

E

Eacott Cl. CV6: Cov 5C 12
Eagle La. CV8: Ken 5D 34
Eagle St. CV1: Cov 5F 19
Eagle St. E. CV1: Cov 5F 19
Earl Pl. Bus. Pk. CV4: Tile H 3F 23
Earl's Croft, The CV3: Cov 5E 25
EARLSDON 4B 24
Earlsdon Av. Nth. CV5: Cov 2B 24
Earlsdon Av. Sth. CV5: Cov 3C 24
Earlsdon Pk. CV1: Cov 5A 4 (2C 24)
Earlsdon St. CV5: Cov 4B 24
Earl St. CV1: Cov 4E 5 (2F 25)
CV12: Bed 4G 7
CV21: Rugby 6H 41
Earls Wlk. CV3: Bin W 2B 36
Easedale Cl. CV3: Cov 6D 24
East Av. CV2: Cov 1A 26
CV12: Bed 4H 7
Eastbourne Cl. CV6: Cov 4A 18
Eastcotes CV4: Tile H 3F 23
Eastern Grn. Rd. CV5: E Grn 1D 22
Easter Way CV7: Ash G 3E 13
Eastfield Pl. CV21: Rugby 6G 41
Eastlands Ct. CV21: Rugby 6A 42
Eastlands Gro. CV5: Cov 6A 18
Eastlands Pl. CV21: Rugby 6B 42
Eastlands Rd. CV21: Rugby 6B 42
Eastleigh Av. CV5: Cov 5B 24
East St. CV1: Cov 3H 5 (1G 25)
CV21: Rugby 5B 42
E. Union St. CV22: Rugby 1G 45
Eastwood Bus. Village
CV3: Bin 3F 27
Eastwood Gro. CV21: Hillm 3G 47
Easy La. CV21: Rugby 6F 41
Eathorpe Cl. CV2: Cov 1C 20
Eaton Rd. CV1: Cov 6C 4 (3E 25)
Ebbw Va. Ter. CV3: Cov 5F 25
Ebourne Cl. CV8: Ken 4E 35
Ebro Cres. CV3: Bin 3F 27
Eburne Rd. CV2: Ald G 5B 14
Eccles Cl. CV2: Cov 2C 20
Ecton Leys CV22: Rugby 4G 45
Edale Way CV6: Cov 3A 20
Eddie Miller Ct. CV12: Bed 4E 7
Eden Cft. CV8: Ken 4F 35
Eden Rd. CV2: Walsg S 1G 21
CV21: Hillm 2D 46
Eden St. CV6: Cov 3H 19
Edgar Wlk. CV2: Cov 4A 20
Edgecote Cl. CV21: Hillm 2D 46
Edgefield Rd. CV2: Walsg S 2G 21
Edgehill Pl. CV4: Tile H 3A 22
EDGWICK 2G 19
Edgwick Rd. CV6: Cov 3H 19
Edinburgh Vs. CV8: Bag 3H 31
Edinburgh Way CV23: Long L 4B 40
Edingale Rd. CV2: Walsg S 2F 21
Edmondson Cl. CV22: Dunc 1D 50
Edmund Rd. CV1: Cov 5F 19
Edward Bailey Cl. CV3: Bin 5E 27
Edward Ct. *CV21: Rugby 6H 41*
(off Railway Ter.)
Edward Rd. CV6: Cov 5C 12
CV12: Bed 3G 7
Edwards Gro. CV8: Ken 3G 35
Edward St. CV6: Cov 5G 19
CV21: Rugby 5F 41
Edward Tyler Rd. CV7: Exh 5E 7
Edwin Cl. CV22: Caw 4A 44
Edyth Rd. CV2: Cov 6E 21
Edyvean Cl. CV22: Bil 5E 45
Egerton Cl. CV21: N'bld A 3F 41
Egret Wlk. CV2: Ald G 5B 14
Elborow St. CV21: Rugby 6G 41
Elderberry Way CV2: Cov 4B 20
Elder Cl. CV22: Bil 2B 44
Eldon Cl. NN6: Crick 2G 49
Eldon Way NN6: Crick 2F 49
Eld Rd. CV6: Cov 3G 19
Electric Wharf CV1: Cov 5E 19
Elgar Rd. CV6: Cov 2B 20
Eliot Ct. CV22: Rugby 6E 41
Elizabeth Way CV2: Walsg S 3F 21
CV8: Ken 3C 34
CV23: Long L 4B 40
Elkington St. CV6: Cov 2H 19
Ellacombe Rd. CV2: Cov 2D 20
Ellenburg Cl. CV4: Tile H 1A 22
Ellen Cl. NN6: Crick 2H 49
Ellerman Gdns. CV6: Longf 5H 13
Ellesmere Rd. CV12: Bed 4E 7

56 A-Z Coventry

Elliott Ct.—Garden Gro.

Elliott Ct. CV5: Cov ... 3G 23
Elliotts Field Retail Pk.
CV21: Rugby ... 2H 41
Ellis Pk. Dr. CV3: Bin ... 3H 27
Ellys Rd. CV1: Cov ... 5E 19
Elmbank Rd. CV8: Ken ... 2C 34
Elm Cl. CV3: Bin W ... 2A 36
Elm Ct. CV5: Alle ... 2A 16
Elmdene Cl. CV8: Wols ... 5E 37
Elmdene Rd. CV8: Ken ... 4F 35
Elmhurst Rd. CV6: Longf ... 4A 14
Elmore Cl. CV3: Bin ... 4D 26
Elmore Rd. CV22: Bil ... 2F 45
Elms, The CV12: Bed ... 4C 6
Elmsdale Av. CV6: Cov ... 6G 13
Elms Dr. CV22: Hillm ... 3D 46
Elms Paddock, The
CV23: Clift D ... 4D 42
Elm Tree Av. CV4: Tile H ... 2E 23
Elm Tree Rd. CV12: Bulk ... 4F 9
Elmwood Av. CV6: Cov ... 5B 18
Elmwood Ct. CV1: Cov ... 1C 4 (6E 19)
Elphin Cl. CV6: Cov ... 5C 12
Elsee Rd. CV21: Rugby ... 6H 41
Elstop Av. CV23: Brow ... 2H 43
Elter Cl. CV21: Brow ... 2B 42
Eltham Rd. CV3: Cov ... 5G 25
Elwy Circ. CV7: Ash G ... 1D 12
Ely Cl. CV2: Walsg S ... 4G 21
Embassy Wlk. CV2: Cov ... 2D 20
Emerson Rd. CV2: Cov ... 1C 26
Emery Cl. CV2: Cov ... 3E 21
Emily Smith Ho. *CV2: Cov ... 1B 20*
(off Roseberry Av.)
Emperor Way CV21: Rugby ... 2F 41
Empire Rd. CV4: Tile H ... 2C 22
Empress Arc. CV3: Cov ... 2B 26
Emscote Rd. CV3: Cov ... 2C 26
Ena Rd. CV1: Cov ... 5F 19
Endemere Rd. CV6: Cov ... 2F 19
Endicott Bend CV4: Tile H ... 1A 22
Enfield Rd. CV2: Cov ... 1B 26
Engleton Rd. CV6: Cov ... 4C 18
Ennerdale CV21: Brow ... 2A 42
Ennerdale La. CV2: Cov ... 6F 21
Ensign Bus. Cen.
CV4: Westw H ... 6D 22
Ensign Cl. CV4: Tile H ... 3B 22
Enterprise Cen.
CV1: Cov ... 6E 5 (3F 25)
Epsom Cl. CV12: Bed ... 2F 7
Epsom Dr. CV3: W'hall ... 6C 26
Epsom Rd. CV22: Bil ... 2D 44
Erica Av. CV12: Bed ... 4D 6
Eric Grey Cl. CV2: Cov ... 5A 20
Eric Inott Ho. CV3: Cov ... 6G 25
Erithway Rd. CV3: Finh ... 2D 30
Ernesford Grange Leisure Cen.
... 4D 26
Ernest Richards Rd.
CV12: Bed ... 2F 7
Ernsford Av. CV3: Cov ... 3B 26
Esher Dr. CV3: Cov ... 5G 25
Eskdale CV21: Brow ... 1A 42
Eskdale Wlk. CV3: W'hall ... 5D 26
Essen La. CV23: Kils ... 5B 48
Essex Cl. CV5: E Grn ... 1F 23
CV8: Ken ... 6C 34
Essex St. CV21: Rugby ... 5G 41
Esterton Cl. CV6: Cov ... 6E 13
Ethelfield Rd. CV2: Cov ... 1B 26
Ettington Rd. CV5: E Grn ... 1E 23
Eustace Rd. CV12: Bulk ... 5F 9
Euston Cres. CV3: W'hall ... 5C 26
Evans Cl. CV12: Bed ... 3G 7
Evans Rd. CV22: Bil ... 1C 44
Evelyn Av. CV6: Cov ... 6G 13
Evenlode Cres. CV6: Cov ... 5B 18
Everard Cl. CV23: Clift D ... 4E 43
Everdon Cl. CV22: Hillm ... 3B 46
Everdon Rd. CV6: Cov ... 6E 13
(not continuous)
Everest Rd. CV22: Rugby ... 3E 45
Evergreen Cl. CV5: Alle ... 1F 17
Eversleigh Rd. CV6: Cov ... 3A 18
Evesham Wlk. CV4: Canly ... 1H 29
Evreux Way CV21: Rugby ... 6G 41
Ewart Pl. CV22: Caw ... 2B 44
Exeter Cl. CV3: Bin ... 4D 26
EXHALL ... 1A 14
Exhall Basin CV6: Longf ... 3B 14
Exhall Grn. CV7: Exh ... 1H 13
EXHALL HALL GREEN ... 1H 13
Exhall Mobile Homes
CV7: Ash G ... 1D 12
Exhall Rd. CV7: Ker E ... 2B 12
Exminster Rd. CV3: Cov ... 1G 31
Exmouth Cl. CV2: Cov ... 3C 20
Exton Cl. CV7: Ash G ... 1E 13
Eydon Cl. CV21: Brow ... 3C 42

F

Fabian Cl. CV3: W'hall ... 5D 26
Fairbanks Cl. CV2: Walsg S ... 3G 21
Fairbourne Way CV6: Cov ... 2A 18
Faircroft CV8: Ken ... 5D 34
Fairfax St. CV1: Cov ... 3E 5 (1F 25)
Fairfield CV7: Exh ... 5E 7
Fairfield Ct. CV3: Cov ... 5A 26
Fairfield Ri. CV7: Mer ... 5A 10
Fairlands Pk. CV4: Canly ... 1A 30
Fairmile Cl. CV3: Bin ... 4C 26
Fairview Wlk. CV6: Longf ... 6G 13
Fairway Ct. CV21: Rugby ... 5B 42
Fairway Ri. CV8: Ken ... 2G 35
Fairways Cl. CV5: Alle ... 4E 17
Falcon Av. CV3: Bin ... 4F 27
Falkener Ho. CV6: Cov ... 3G 19
Falkland Cl. CV4: Tile H ... 5B 22
Fallow Fld. Cl. CV22: Caw ... 2B 44
Fallowfields CV6: Cov ... 4D 12
NN6: Crick ... 2H 49
Falstaff Dr. CV22: Bil ... 6D 44
Falstaff Rd. CV4: Tile H ... 2C 22
Fancott Dr. CV8: Ken ... 2D 34
Faraday Rd. CV22: Rugby ... 2A 46
Farber Rd. CV2: Walsg S ... 4G 21
Farcroft Av. CV5: E Grn ... 6B 16
Fareham Av. CV22: Hillm ... 3C 46
Far Gosford St.
CV1: Cov ... 4G 5 (2G 25)
Farlow Cl. CV6: Cov ... 4A 20
Farman Rd. CV5: Cov ... 2B 24
Farm Cl. CV6: Cov ... 5D 12
Farmcote Lodge *CV2: Ald G ... 4B 14*
(off Farmcote Rd.)
Farmcote Rd. CV2: Ald G ... 4B 14
Farmers Ct. *CV21: Rugby ... 5A 42*
(off Gavel Dr.)
Farmer Ward Rd. CV8: Ken ... 4E 35
Farm Gro. CV22: Rugby ... 2A 46
Farm Pl. CV3: Cov ... 4C 26
Farm Rd. CV8: Ken ... 6C 34
Farmside CV3: W'hall ... 1D 32
Farmstead, The CV3: Cov ... 4B 26
Farnborough Av. CV22: Rugby ... 1E 45
Farndale Av. CV6: Cov ... 5F 13
Farndon Cl. CV12: Bulk ... 3D 8
Farr Dr. CV4: Tile H ... 2F 23
Farren Rd. CV2: Cov ... 6D 20
Farthing Ct. CV21: Hillm ... 3F 47
Farthing Wlk. CV4: Westw H ... 6B 22
Faseman Av. CV4: Tile H ... 1D 22
Faulconbridge Av. CV5: E Grn ... 6C 16
Fawley Cl. CV3: W'hall ... 6D 26
Fawsley Leys CV22: Rugby ... 4G 45
Faygate Cl. CV3: Bin ... 1G 27
Featherbed La. CV4: Westw H ... 1E 29
CV21: Hillm ... 3E 47
Fein Bank CV4: Tile H ... 2A 22
Fellows Way CV21: Hillm ... 4D 46
Felton Cl. CV2: Walsg S ... 1E 21
Fennell Ho. CV1: Cov ... 4A 4
Fennyland La. CV8: Ken ... 1F 35
Fenside Av. CV3: Cov ... 2F 31
Fenton Rd. CV5: Alle ... 2F 17
Fenwick Cl. CV6: Cov ... 1G 19
Fenwick Dr. CV21: Hillm ... 3E 47
Fern Cl. CV2: Cov ... 6C 14
CV23: Brow ... 1B 42
Ferndale Dr. CV8: Ken ... 6E 35
Ferndale Rd. CV3: Bin W ... 2B 36
Ferndown Cl. CV4: Tile H ... 1D 22
Ferndown Ct. CV22: Bil ... 2E 45
Ferndown Rd. CV22: Bil ... 2E 45
Ferndown Ter. CV22: Bil ... 2E 45
Fern Gro. CV12: Bed ... 4C 6
Fernhill Cl. CV8: Ken ... 2C 34
Ferrers Cl. CV4: Tile H ... 2D 22
Ferriby Rd. CV22: Caw ... 3B 44
Ferrieres Cl. CV22: Dunc ... 2C 50
Fetherston Cres. CV8: Rytn D ... 5H 33
Field Cl. CV8: Ken ... 3F 35
Field Ct. CV2: Cov ... 3C 20
Fieldfare Cl. CV23: Brow ... 1A 42
Fieldgate La. CV8: Ken ... 2C 34
Fieldgate Lawn CV8: Ken ... 2D 34
Fielding Cl. CV2: Walsg S ... 4G 21
Field March CV3: W'hall ... 1E 33
Fieldside La. CV3: Bin ... 1F 27
Field Vw. CV22: Caw ... 3B 44
Field Vw. Cl. CV7: Exh ... 6E 7
Fife Rd. CV5: Cov ... 2B 24
Fillongley Rd. CV7: Mer ... 5A 10
Finbarr Cl. CV6: Cov ... 5G 19
Finch Cl. CV6: Cov ... 6E 13
Findon Cl. CV12: Bulk ... 3E 9
Fingal Cl. CV3: W'hall ... 6C 26
Fingest Cl. CV5: Cov ... 6F 17
FINHAM ... 3E 31
Finham Cres. CV8: Ken ... 2F 35
Finham Flats CV8: Ken ... 2F 35
Finham Grn. Rd. CV3: Finh ... 3D 30
Finham Gro. CV3: Finh ... 3E 31
Finham Pk. CV3: Finh ... 4E 31
Finham Rd. CV8: Ken ... 2F 35
Finlay Ct. CV1: Cov ... 6D 4 (3F 25)
Finmere CV21: Brow ... 3B 42
Finnemore Cl. CV3: Cov ... 1D 30
Firedrake Cft.
CV1: Cov ... 5H 5 (2H 25)
Fir Gro. CV4: Tile H ... 2E 23
Firleigh Dr. CV12: Bulk ... 3F 9
(not continuous)
Firs, The CV5: Cov ... 4C 24
CV7: Mer ... 5A 10
CV12: Bed ... 4C 6
Firs Dr. CV22: Rugby ... 1F 45
Firs Est. CV5: Cov ... 4D 24
First Av. CV3: Cov ... 3C 26
Fir Tree Av. CV4: Tile H ... 2E 23
Fisher Av. CV22: Hillm ... 3C 46
Fisher Rd. CV6: Cov ... 2G 19
Fishers Cl. CV23: Kils ... 6B 48
Fishponds Rd. CV8: Ken ... 5C 34
Fitness First for Women
Coventry, Bishop St.
... 2D 4 (1E 25)
Coventry, De Montfort Way
... 6G 23
Fitzalan Cl. CV23: Chu L ... 3D 38
Fitzroy Cl. CV2: Walsg S ... 4H 21
Fivefield Rd. CV7: Ker E ... 3H 11
Flamborough Cl. CV3: Bin ... 4F 27
Flaunden Cl. CV5: Cov ... 6F 17
Flaxdown Gdns. *CV23: Brow ... 2H 43*
(off Tower Furlong)
Flecknose St. CV3: W'hall ... 6C 26
Fleet Cres. CV21: Hillm ... 1C 46
Fleet Ho. CV1: Cov ... 4C 4 (2E 25)
Fleet St. CV1: Cov ... 3C 4 (1E 25)
Fletchamstead Highway
CV4: Cov ... 2G 23
Fletchamstead Highway Ind. Est.
CV4: Cov ... 5H 23
Fletcher Wlk. CV3: Finh ... 2E 31
Fletchworth Ga. CV5: Cov ... 4H 23
Fletchworth Ga. Ind. Est.
CV5: Cov ... 4G 23
Florence Cl. CV12: Bed ... 6D 6
Florence Rd. CV3: Bin ... 2G 27
Florin Cl. CV4: Westw H ... 6C 22
Florin Pl. CV21: Hillm ... 3E 47
Flowerdale Dr. CV2: Cov ... 4B 20
Flude Rd. CV7: Ash G ... 2E 13
Flynt Av. CV5: Alle ... 4E 17
FOLESHILL ... 1A 20
Foleshill Ent. Pk. CV6: Cov ... 4F 19
Foleshill Leisure Cen. ... 3F 19
Foleshill Rd. CV1: Cov ... 1D 4 (5F 19)
CV6: Cov ... 5F 19
Folkland Grn. CV6: Cov ... 3B 18
Follager Rd. CV21: Rugby ... 5E 41
Follis Wlk. CV4: Westw H ... 6B 22
Fontmell Cl. CV2: Walsg S ... 6G 21
Forders La. CV12: Bulk ... 1B 8
Ford St. CV1: Cov ... 2F 5 (1F 25)
Fordwell Cl. CV5: Cov ... 1B 24
Foreland Way CV6: Cov ... 5C 12
Foresters Pl. CV21: Hillm ... 4F 47
Foresters Rd. CV3: Cov ... 6G 25
Forfield Rd. CV6: Cov ... 4A 18
Forge Rd. CV8: Ken ... 2E 35
Forge Way CV6: Cov ... 5E 13
Forknell Av. CV2: Cov ... 5C 20
Fornside Cl. CV21: Brow ... 2B 42
Forrest Rd. CV8: Ken ... 4C 34
Forsythia Cl. CV12: Bed ... 4B 6
Fosse, The CV8: Wols ... 5G 37
Fosse Way CV23: Bret ... 4H 37
(Bunkers Hill La.)
CV23: Bret ... 2A 38
(Queens Rd.)
Fosseway Rd. CV3: Finh ... 2D 30
Fosterd Rd. CV21: N'bld A ... 4F 41
Foster Rd. CV6: Cov ... 3C 18
Founder Cl. CV4: Tile H ... 4D 22
FOUR LANES END ... 4C 6
Four Pounds Av. CV5: Cov ... 1B 24
Fowler Rd. CV6: Cov ... 1A 4 (5D 18)
Fow Oak CV4: Tile H ... 2A 22
Fox Cl. CV21: Hillm ... 2F 47
Foxfield Pl. CV23: Long L ... 5A 40
FOXFORD ... 4A 14
Foxford Cres. CV2: Ald G ... 4B 14
Foxford Leisure Cen. ... 3B 14
Foxglove Cl. CV6: Cov ... 6E 13
CV12: Bed ... 5C 6
CV23: Brow ... 1C 42
Foxon's Barn Rd. CV21: Brow ... 3A 42
Foxton Rd. CV3: Bin ... 3E 27
Foxwood Dr. CV3: Bin W ... 2B 36
Framlingham Gro. CV8: Ken ... 2G 35
Frampton Wlk. CV2: Walsg S ... 6F 21
Frances Cres. CV12: Bed ... 3E 7
Frances Rd. CV8: Bag ... 3G 31
Franciscan Rd. CV3: Cov ... 4E 25
Francis Dr. CV22: Caw ... 3A 44
Francis St. CV6: Cov ... 3G 19
Frankland Rd. CV6: Cov ... 1A 20
Franklin Gro. CV4: Tile H ... 3C 22
Franklins Gdns. CV3: Bin ... 3H 27
Frankpledge Rd. CV3: Cov ... 5G 25
Frankton Av. CV3: Cov ... 1E 31
Frank Walsh Ho. CV1: Cov ... 6F 19
Frankwell Dr. CV2: Walsg S ... 1E 21
Fraser Rd. CV6: Cov ... 1C 18
Frederick Neal Av. CV5: E Grn ... 6B 16
Frederick Press Way
CV21: Rugby ... 6F 41
Frederick St. CV21: Rugby ... 6F 41
Fred Lee Gro. CV3: Cov ... 2F 31
Freeburn C'way. CV4: Canly ... 5G 23
Freehold St. CV1: Cov ... 5H 19
Freeman St. CV6: Cov ... 4H 19
Freeman's Way
CV1: Cov ... 5C 4 (2E 25)
Freemantle Rd. CV22: Bil ... 1C 44
Freshfield Cl. CV5: Alle ... 1G 17
Fretton Cl. CV6: Cov ... 3H 19
Frevill Rd. CV6: Cov ... 2B 20
Frewen Rd. CV22: Caw ... 3A 44
Friars Cl. CV3: Bin W ... 2C 36
Friars Rd. CV1: Cov ... 6D 4 (2E 25)
Friends Cl. CV8: Bag ... 3F 31
Friesian Ct. *CV21: Rugby ... 5H 41*
(off Gavel Dr.)
Frilsham Way CV5: Cov ... 6F 17
Frisby Rd. CV4: Tile H ... 2C 22
Friswell Dr. CV6: Cov ... 2H 19
Friswell Ho. CV2: Cov ... 2D 20
Frobisher Rd. CV3: Cov ... 1E 31
CV22: Bil ... 2C 44
Frogmere Cl. CV5: Alle ... 4F 17
Frythe Cl. CV8: Ken ... 2G 35
Fuchsia Cl. CV2: Cov ... 6B 14
Fulbrook Rd. CV2: Cov ... 1C 20
Fullers Cl. CV6: Cov ... 3B 18
Fullwood Cl. CV2: Ald G ... 6E 15
Fulmer Cl. CV2: Ald G ... 5B 14
Furlong Rd. CV1: Cov ... 6F 5 (3F 25)
Furnace Cl. CV12: Bed ... 2H 7
Furnace Rd. CV12: Bed ... 2H 7
Furness Cl. CV21: Brow ... 2B 42
Furrow Cl. CV21: Rugby ... 5B 42
Fusiliers Cl. CV3: Cov ... 3A 26
Futures Wlk. CV3: W'hall ... 6D 26
Fylde Ho. CV2: Cov ... 6D 20
Fynford Rd. CV6: Cov ... 5D 18

G

Gable Cl. CV22: Bil ... 3D 44
Gabor Cl. CV21: Rugby ... 3A 42
Gainford Ri. CV3: Bin ... 1F 27
Gainsborough Cres.
CV21: Hillm ... 2F 47
Gainsborough Dr. CV12: Bed ... 2E 7
Gala Bingo
Coventry, Brade Dr. ... 3H 21
Coventry, Fairfax St.
... 3F 5 (1F 25)
Coventry, Radford Rd. ... 4D 18
Rugby ... 6G 41
Galey's Rd. CV3: Cov ... 4F 25
Gallagher Bus. Pk.
CV6: Longf ... 3G 13
Gallagher Retail Pk. CV6: Cov ... 2H 19
Gallagher Rd. CV12: Bed ... 4E 7
Gallagher Way CV6: Cov ... 3H 19
Galliards, The CV4: Canly ... 2H 29
Galloway M. *CV21: Rugby ... 5H 41*
(off Craven Rd.)
Galmington Dr. CV3: Cov ... 6D 24
Gamecock Barracks
CV11: Bram ... 1H 9
Gardeners End CV22: Rugby ... 1D 44
Garden Flats CV5: E Grn ... 5B 16
Garden Gro. CV12: Bed ... 6D 6

A-Z Coventry 57

Gardenia Dr.—Hazlemere Cl.

Gardenia Dr. CV5: Alle 4E 17
Gardens, The CV8: Ken 5E 35
CV23: Thurl 5A 50
Gardner Ho. CV1: Cov 4A 4
Gardner Way CV8: Ken 6E 35
Garlands Cft. CV7: Ker E 2C 12
Garlick Dr. CV8: Ken 2G 35
Garratt Cl. CV23: Long L 4B 40
Garrick Cl. CV5: E Grn 6A 16
Garth Cres. CV3: Bin 4D 26
Garth Ho. CV3: Bin 5D 26
Garyth Williams Cl. CV22: Bil 3E 45
Gas St. CV21: Rugby 6H 41
Gatehouse Cl. CV21: Hillm 3E 47
Gatehouse La. CV12: Bed 4E 7
Gateside Rd. CV6: Cov 6G 13
Gaulby Wlk. CV3: Bin 3G 27
Gavel Dr. CV21: Rugby 5H 41
Gaveston Rd. CV6: Cov 4A 18
Gaydon Cl. CV6: Cov 2A 20
Gayer St. CV6: Cov 1A 20
Gayhurst Cl. CV3: Bin 4E 27
Gaza Cl. CV4: Tile H 3E 23
Gazelle Cl. CV1: Cov 2G 5 (1G 25)
Generator Hall *CV1: Cov 5E 19*
(off Electric Wharf)
Gentian Way CV23: Brow 1C 42
Geoffrey Cl. CV2: Cov 5B 20
George Eliot Av. CV12: Bed 4H 7
George Eliot Rd. CV1: Cov 5F 19
George Hodgkinson Cl.
CV4: Tile H 1D 22
George Marston Rd. CV3: Bin 3E 27
George Pk. Cl. CV2: Cov 1C 20
George Poole Ho. *CV1: Cov 4A 4*
(off Windsor St.)
George Robertson Cl.
CV3: Bin 5E 27
George Row CV23: Kils 5C 48
George St. CV1: Cov 5F 19
CV12: Bed 3F 7
CV21: Rugby 6F 41
George St. Ringway CV12: Bed 3F 7
Gerard Av. CV4: Canly 4F 23
Gerard Ct. CV22: Caw 3A 44
Gerard Pl. CV22: Caw 3A 44
Gerard Rd. CV22: Caw 3A 44
Gerard Row CV22: Caw 3A 44
GIBBET HILL 4H 29
Gibbet Hill Rd. CV4: Canly 1F 29
Gibbons Cl. CV4: Tile H 2D 22
Gibbs Cl. CV2: Walsg S 4H 21
Gibraltar Cl. CV3: Cov 3H 25
Gibson Cres. CV12: Bed 5E 7
Gibson Dr. CV21: Hillm 2E 47
Gielgud Way CV2: Walsg S 2H 21
Giffard Wlk. *CV22: Caw 3A 44*
(off Frewen Rd.)
Gilbert Av. CV22: Bil 1D 44
Gilbert Cl. CV1: Cov 2H 5 (1G 25)
CV12: Bed 5F 7
Gilbert Horal Cl. CV4: Tile H 4D 22
Giles Cl. CV6: Cov 6E 13
Gillian's Wlk. CV2: Walsg S 2G 21
Gillquart Way CV1: Cov 3F 25
Gingles Ct. CV21: Hillm 3E 47
Girdlers Cl. CV3: Cov 1D 30
Girtin Cl. CV12: Bed 2E 7
Givens Ho. CV1: Cov 4A 4
Glade, The CV5: E Grn 1D 22
Gladiator Way CV21: Rugby 2F 41
Gladstone St. CV21: Rugby 5F 41
Glaisdale Av. CV6: Cov 5G 13
Glamorgan Cl. CV3: W'hall 1D 32
Glaramara Cl. CV21: Brow 2B 42
Glasshouse La. CV8: Ken 3G 35
Glebe, The CV7: Cor 1G 11
Glebe Av. CV12: Bed 5C 6
Glebe Cl. CV4: Tile H 5E 23
Glebe Cres. CV8: Ken 5E 35
CV21: Rugby 6E 41
Glebefarm Gro. CV3: Bin 1F 27
Glebe Farm Ind. Est.
CV21: Rugby 2F 41
Glebe Farm Rd. CV21: Rugby 2F 41
Glencoe Rd. CV3: Cov 2B 26
Glendale Av. CV8: Ken 2E 35
Glendale Way CV4: Tile H 2A 22
Glendon Gdns. CV12: Bulk 3E 9
Glendower Av. CV5: Cov 2H 23
Gleneagles Rd. CV2: Cov 4E 21
Glenfern Gdns. CV8: Rytn D 4E 33
Glenmore Dr. CV6: Longf 3H 13
Glenmount Av. CV6: Longf 3H 13
Glenn St. CV6: Cov 5F 13
Glenridding Cl. CV6: Longf 3H 13
Glenrosa Wlk. CV4: Tile H 5E 23
Glenroy Cl. CV2: Cov 4E 21
Glentworth Av. CV6: Cov 6C 12
Glenwood Gdns. CV12: Bed 2E 7
Gloster Dr. CV8: Ken 2D 34
Gloucester St.
CV1: Cov 3A 4 (1D 24)
Glovers Cl. CV7: Mer 5A 10
Glover St. CV3: Cov 4F 25
Goals Soccer Cen. AT7
Coventry 3A 20
Godiva Lodge CV2: Cov 5A 20
Godiva Pl. CV1: Cov 3G 5 (1G 25)
Godiva Trad. Est. CV6: Cov 2H 19
Gold Av. CV22: Caw 3B 44
Golden Acres La. CV3: Bin 5F 27
Goldsmith Av. CV22: Rugby 4F 45
Goldthorn Cl. CV5: E Grn 6B 16
Goodacre Cl. CV23: Clift D 4E 43
Goode Cft. CV4: Tile H 2D 22
Goodman Way CV4: Tile H 3A 22
Goodwood Cl. CV3: W'hall 6C 26
GOODYERS END 6A 6
Goodyers End La. CV12: Bed 6A 6
Gordon Cl. CV12: Bed 2F 7
Gordon St. CV1: Cov 6A 4 (3C 24)
Goring Rd. CV2: Cov 6A 20
Gorse Cl. CV22: Bil 2E 45
Gorseway CV5: Cov 1G 23
GOSFORD GREEN 2H 25
Gosford Ind. Est.
CV1: Cov 4H 5 (2H 25)
Gosford St. CV1: Cov 4F 5 (2F 25)
Gospel Oak Rd. CV6: Cov 4D 12
Gosport Rd. CV6: Cov 2G 19
Gossett La. CV8: Bran 2C 36
Grafton Cl. CV8: Ken 5E 35
Grafton Ct. CV4: Canly 5F 23
Grafton St. CV1: Cov 4H 5 (2G 25)
Graham Cl. CV6: Cov 1B 20
Graham Rd. CV21: Rugby 5A 42
Gramercy Pk. CV4: Tile H 1A 22
Granborough Cl. CV3: Bin 4F 27
Grandsire Dr. CV21: Hillm 3E 47
Grange Av. CV3: Bin 5F 27
CV3: Finh 3E 31
CV8: Ken 1C 34
Grangemouth Rd. CV6: Cov 4D 18
Grange Rd. CV6: Longf 4A 14
CV21: N'bld A 3E 41
Grange Wlk. CV6: Longf 3B 14
Granoe Cl. CV3: Bin 4E 27
Grantham St. CV2: Cov 1H 25
Grant Rd. CV3: Cov 2B 26
CV7: Exh 6E 7
Grapes Cl. CV6: Cov 5D 18
Grasmere Av. CV3: Cov 6B 24
Grasmere Cl. CV21: Brow 3B 42
Grasmere Rd. CV12: Bed 4F 7
Grasscroft Dr. CV3: Cov 6G 25
Gratton Ct. CV3: Cov 6B 24
Gravel Hill CV4: Tile H 3C 22
Graylands, The CV3: Finh 2E 31
Grays Orchard CV23: Thurl 6A 50
Grayswood Av. CV5: Cov 6H 17
Great Borne CV21: Brow 1A 42
Gt. Central Way CV21: Rugby 5B 42
Gt. Central Way Ind. Est.
CV21: Rugby 4B 42
GREAT HEATH 4G 19
Green, The CV7: Mer 5A 10
CV22: Bil 3C 44
CV22: Dunc 2C 50
CV23: Long L 5A 40
Green Cl. CV23: Long L 5H 39
Green Ct. CV21: Rugby 5B 42
Greendale Rd. CV5: Cov 1H 23
Greenfield, The CV3: Cov 4B 26
Greenfinch Ct. CV2: Cov 2C 20
Greenhill Rd. CV22: Bil 2F 45
Greenland Av. CV5: Alle 5D 16
Greenland Ct. CV5: Alle 5D 16
GREEN LANE 2D 30
Green La. CV3: Cov, Finh 6C 24
CV3: Finh 2D 30
CV7: Cor 2B 10
CV8: Bran 2D 36
CV23: Chu L 4E 39
Greenleaf Cl. CV5: E Grn 1E 23
Greenodd Dr. CV6: Longf 3H 13
Greensleeves Cl. CV6: Cov 6D 12
Green's Rd. CV6: Cov 1C 18
Greensward, The CV3: Bin 2G 27
Greensward Cl. CV8: Ken 2F 35
Greens Yd. CV12: Bed 3F 7
Greenways CV4: Tile H 2A 22
Greenwood Cl. CV23: Long L 4A 40
Gregory Av. CV3: Cov 6C 24
Gregory Hood Rd. CV3: Cov 1F 31
Grenadier Dr. CV3: Cov 4H 25
Grendon Cl. CV4: Tile H 3A 22
Grendon Dr. CV21: Brow 2C 42
Grenville Av. CV2: Cov 1B 26
Grenville Cl. CV22: Bil 2C 44
Gresham St. CV2: Cov 2A 26
Gresley Rd. CV2: Cov 3D 20
Gressingham Gro. CV6: Cov 3F 19
Greswold Cl. CV4: Tile H 3D 22
Gretna Rd. CV3: Finh 2B 30
Greville Rd. CV8: Ken 4D 34
Greycoat Rd. CV6: Cov 6C 12
Greyfriars Ct. CV6: Cov 3C 18
Greyfriars La.
CV1: Cov 5D 4 (2E 25)
Greyfriars Rd.
CV1: Cov 5C 4 (2E 25)
Griffin Centre, The 6H 41
Griffiths Ho. *CV21: Brow 2A 42*
(off Dovedale Cl.)
Grimston Cl. CV3: Bin 2G 27
Grindal Pl. CV22: Caw 3A 44
Grindle Rd. CV6: Longf 4H 13
Grindley Ho. *CV1: Cov 4A 4*
(off Windsor St.)
Grizebeck Dr. CV5: Alle 5E 17
Grizedale CV21: Brow 2A 42
Grosvenor Ho.
CV1: Cov 6B 4 (2D 24)
Grosvenor Lwr. Rd.
CV1: Cov 6B 4 (3D 24)
Grosvenor Rd.
CV1: Cov 6B 4 (3D 24)
CV21: Rugby 6H 41
Grounds Farm La. CV8: Ken 4B 34
Grove, The CV12: Bed 3F 7
Grove Ct. CV5: Cov 4D 24
Grove Farm La. CV7: Ker E 5H 11
Grovelands Ind. Est. CV7: Exh 2A 14
Grove La. CV7: Ker E 1B 12
Grove St. CV1: Cov 3F 5 (1F 25)
Guardhouse Rd. CV6: Cov 2D 18
Guildford Ct. CV6: Cov 3F 19
Guild Rd. CV6: Cov 3F 19
Guilsborough Rd. CV3: Bin 4E 27
Guinea Cres. CV4: Westw H 6B 22
Gulson Rd. CV1: Cov 5G 5 (2G 25)
Gun La. CV2: Cov 5A 20
Gunton Av. CV3: W'hall 6C 26
Guphill Av. CV5: Cov 1H 23
Gurney Cl. CV4: Tile H 1C 22
Gutteridge Av. CV6: Cov 6C 12
Guy Rd. CV8: Ken 6D 34
Guys Comn. CV22: Dunc 2D 50
Gypsy La. CV8: Ken 6D 34

H

Haddon End CV3: Cov 6G 25
Haddon St. CV6: Cov 2A 20
Hadfield Cl. CV23: Clift D 4E 43
Hadleigh Rd. CV3: Finh 3E 31
Hadrians Way CV21: Rugby 2F 41
Haig Ct. CV22: Bil 2E 45
Hales Ind. Pk. CV6: Longf 4G 13
Hales St. CV1: Cov 2D 4 (1E 25)
(not continuous)
Halford La. CV6: Cov 1C 18
Halford Lodge CV6: Cov 6C 12
Halfway La. CV22: Dunc 2B 50
Halifax Cl. CV5: Alle 3E 17
Hallam Rd. CV6: Cov 5D 12
Hallam's Cl. CV8: Bran 4D 36
Hallbrook Rd. CV6: Cov 5C 12
Hall Cl. CV23: Kils 5C 48
Hall Close, The CV22: Dunc 3C 50
Hall Dr. CV8: Bag 3G 31
HALL GREEN 6B 14
Hall Grn. Rd. CV6: Cov 6B 14
Hall La. CV2: Walsg S 4F 21
Hamilton Cl. CV12: Bed 5A 6
Hamilton Rd. CV2: Cov 1A 26
Hamlet Cl. CV22: Bil 5D 44
Hammersley St. CV12: Bed 5C 6
Hammond Rd. CV2: Cov 6H 19
Hammonds Ter. CV8: Ken 3B 34
Hampden Way CV22: Bil 4C 44
Hampshire Cl. CV3: Bin 4F 27
Hampton Cl. CV6: Cov 4H 19
Hampton La. CV7: Mer 5A 10
Hampton Rd. CV6: Cov 4H 19
Hanbury Pl. CV6: Cov 6A 14
Hanbury Rd. CV12: Bed 2G 7
Hancock Grn. CV4: Tile H 4D 22
Handcross Gro. CV3: Finh 1C 30
Handleys Cl. CV8: Rytn D 5G 33
Handsworth Cres. CV5: E Grn 6C 16
Hanford Cl. CV6: Cov 4G 19
Hanford Cl. Ind. Est. CV6: Cov 4G 19
Hanover Gdns. CV21: Rugby 5H 41
Hans Cl. CV2: Cov 6H 19
Hanson Way CV6: Longf 4A 14
Hanwood Cl. CV5: E Grn 6A 16
Harborough Rd. CV6: Cov 6D 12
CV23: Harb M 1C 40
Harbourne Cl. CV8: Ken 3E 35
Harcourt CV3: W'hall 1E 33
Hardwick Cl. CV5: E Grn 6E 17
Hardwyn Cl. CV3: Bin 3H 27
Hardy Cl. CV22: Bil 1C 44
Hardy Rd. CV6: Cov 3C 18
Harebell Way CV23: Brow 1B 42
Harefield Ho. CV2: Cov 1B 26
Harefield Rd. CV2: Cov 1B 26
Harewood Rd. CV5: Cov 1G 23
Harger Ct. CV8: Ken 4D 34
Harger M. CV8: Ken 4D 34
Hargrave Cl. CV3: Bin 3G 27
Harington Rd. CV6: Cov 5C 18
Harlech Cl. CV8: Ken 3G 35
Harley St. CV2: Cov 1A 26
Harlow Wlk. CV2: Walsg S 3G 21
Harmer Cl. CV2: Walsg S 3G 21
Harnall La. CV1: Cov 6F 19
Harnall La. E. CV1: Cov 1F 5 (6F 19)
Harnall La. Ind. Est. CV1: Cov 6F 19
Harnall La. W. CV1: Cov 6F 19
Harnall Row CV1: Cov 3H 5 (1G 25)
(not continuous)
Harold Cox Pl. CV22: Bil 5E 45
Harold Rd. CV2: Cov 2D 26
Harpenden Dr. CV5: Alle 5E 17
Harper Rd. CV1: Cov 5G 5 (2G 25)
Harris Dr. CV22: Rugby 3F 45
Harrison Cl. CV21: Hillm 3F 47
Harrison Cres. CV12: Bed 4E 7
Harris Rd. CV3: Cov 2B 26
Harrow Cl. CV6: Longf 4A 14
Harry Caplan Ho. CV5: Alle 4F 17
Harry Edwards Ho. CV2: Cov 2D 20
Harry Rose Rd. CV2: Cov 1E 27
Harry Salt Ho. CV1: Cov 2G 5
Harry Stanley Ho. CV6: Cov 2A 20
Harry Truslove Cl. CV6: Cov 3C 18
Harry Weston Rd. CV3: Bin 3F 27
Hart Cl. CV21: Hillm 1B 46
Hartington Cres. CV5: Cov 3A 24
Hartland Av. CV2: Cov 4B 20
Hartlepool Rd. CV1: Cov 6G 19
Hartridge Wlk. CV5: Cov 6F 17
Harvesters Cl. CV3: Bin 2G 27
Harvest Hill La. CV5: Alle 3A 10
CV7: Mer 3A 10
Harvey Cl. CV5: Alle 3E 17
Harvon Gth. CV21: Rugby 5A 42
Haselbech Rd. CV3: Bin 3F 27
Haseley Rd. CV2: Cov 1C 20
Hasilwood Sq. CV3: Cov 2B 26
Hastings Rd. CV2: Cov 6A 20
Haswell Cl. CV22: Rugby 1A 46
Hathaway Rd. CV4: Tile H 3B 22
Hatters Ct. CV12: Bed 4G 7
Havendale Cl. CV6: Cov 5D 18
HAWKESBURY 2B 14
Hawkesbury Golf Course 1B 14
HAWKES END 6G 11
Hawkeshead CV21: Brow 2B 42
Hawkes Mill La. CV5: Alle 6E 11
Hawkesworth Dr. CV8: Ken 2E 35
Hawkins Cl. CV22: Bil 2E 45
Hawkins Rd. CV5: Cov 2C 24
Hawksworth Dr.
CV1: Cov 2A 4 (1C 24)
Hawlands CV21: Brow 3A 42
Hawthorn Ct. CV4: Tile H 2C 22
Hawthorne Cl. CV8: Wols 5E 37
Hawthorn La. CV4: Tile H 1C 22
(Delius St.)
CV4: Tile H 2C 22
(Roosevelt Dr.)
Hawthorn Way CV22: Bil 2B 44
Haydock Cl. CV6: Ald G 4B 14
Hayes Cl. CV21: Brow 2B 42
Hayes Grn. Rd. CV12: Bed 5D 6
Hayes La. CV7: Exh 6D 6
Hay La. CV1: Cov 4E 5 (2F 25)
Haynestone Rd. CV6: Cov 4A 18
Haynes Way CV21: Rugby 1F 41
Hayton Grn. CV4: Tile H 4D 22
(not continuous)
Haytor Ri. CV2: Cov 3C 20
Haywards Grn. CV6: Cov 3C 18
Hazel Gro. CV12: Bed 3H 7
Hazel Rd. CV6: Cov 1B 20
Hazelwood Cl. CV22: Dunc 2B 50
Hazlemere Cl. CV5: Cov 6F 17

Headborough Rd. CV2: Cov 5A 20
Headington Av. CV6: Cov 6C 12
Headlands, The CV5: Cov 6H 17
Healey Cl. CV21: Brow 2A 42
Health Cen. Rd. CV4: Canly 2G 29
Hearsall Comn. CV2: Cov 2A 24
Hearsall Ct. CV5: Cov 2H 23
Hearsall La. CV5: Cov 2B 24
Heart Park 1A 10
HEATH 1C 50
Heath, The CV22: Dunc 2C 50
Heath Av. CV12: Bed 5C 6
Heathcote St. CV6: Cov 4C 18
Heath Cres. CV2: Cov 4C 18
Heather Cl. CV22: Bil 2E 45
Heather Dr. CV12: Bed 4C 6
Heather Rd. CV2: Cov 6B 14
  CV3: Bin W 2A 36
Heathfield Rd. CV5: Cov 2G 23
Heath Grn. Way
  CV4: Westw H 6D 22
Heathlands, The
  CV23: Clift D 4E 43
Heath La. CV23: Brin 1G 37
Heath Rd. CV2: Cov 6H 19
  CV12: Bed 5D 6
Heath Way CV22: Hillm 3B 46
Heckley Rd. CV7: Exh 1A 14
Heddle Gro. CV6: Cov 2B 20
Hedgefield Way CV4: Tile H 4D 22
Hedgerow Wlk. CV6: Cov 4D 12
Heera Cl. CV6: Cov 3F 19
Helen St. CV6: Cov 4H 19
Hele Rd. CV3: Cov 6F 25
Helmdon Cl. CV21: Brow 3B 42
Helvellyn Way CV21: Brow 2B 42
Hemingford Rd. CV2: Walsg S 2G 21
Hemsby Cl. CV4: Canly 5E 23
Hemsworth Dr. CV12: Bulk 4D 8
Henderson Cl. CV5: Alle 3G 17
Hendre Cl. CV5: Cov 2G 23
Hen La. CV6: Cov 5E 13
Henley Ct. CV2: Cov 3D 20
HENLEY GREEN 2D 20
Henley Ind. Pk. CV2: Cov 3E 21
Henley Mill La. CV2: Cov 3B 20
Henley Rd. CV2: Cov, Walsg S 1B 20
Henley Wlk. CV2: Cov 2D 20
Henrietta St. CV6: Cov 5G 19
Henry Boteler Rd. CV4: Canly 5F 23
Henry St. CV1: Cov 2D 4 (1E 25)
  CV8: Ken 3E 35
  CV21: Rugby 6G 41
Henson Rd. CV12: Bed 5C 6
Hepworth Rd. CV3: Bin 2H 27
Herald Av. CV5: Cov 3G 23
Herald Bus. Pk. CV3: Bin 5F 27
Herald Way CV3: Bin 5G 27
Herbert Art Gallery & Museum, The
  ....4E 5 (2F 25)
Herberts La. CV8: Ken 3E 35
Herders Way CV7: Ker E 2B 12
Herdwick Ct. CV21: Rugby 5H 41
  (off Murray Rd.)
Hereford Cl. CV21: Rugby 5H 41
Heritage Cl. CV4: Canly 3H 29
Heritage Dr. CV6: Longf 2C 14
Hermes Cres. CV2: Cov 3D 20
Hermitage Rd. CV2: Cov 6C 20
Hermitage Way CV8: Ken 5E 35
Hermit's Cft. CV3: Cov 4F 25
Heronbank CV4: Tile H 2A 22
Heron Ho. CV2: Cov 1B 26
Herrick Rd. CV2: Cov 6H 19
Hertford Pl. CV1: Cov 5B 4 (2D 24)
Hertford St. CV1: Cov 4D 4 (2E 25)
Heslop Cl. CV3: Bin 4F 27
Hever Hall CV1: Cov 3G 5
Hewitt Av. CV6: Cov 1A 4 (5D 18)
Hexby Cl. CV4: Walsg S 4G 21
Hexworthy Av. CV3: Cov 1D 30
Heybrook Cl. CV2: Cov 3C 20
Heycroft CV4: Canly 2H 29
Heyford Cl. CV2: Ald G 5D 14
Heyford Leys CV22: Rugby 5F 45
Heyville Cft. CV8: Ken 5G 35
Heywood Cl. CV6: Cov 3A 20
Hibberd Ct. CV8: Ken 4D 34
Hibbert Cl. CV22: Rugby 2F 45
Hickory Cl. CV2: Walsg S 1F 21
Hidcote Cl. CV21: Rugby 1E 45
Hidcote Ho. CV4: Tile H 5B 22
Hidcote Rd. CV8: Ken 2G 35
High Ash Cl. CV7: Exh 1H 13
High Beech CV5: Alle 4E 17
Highbury Cl. CV7: Mer 5A 10
Highfield Cl. CV8: Ken 4C 34
Highfield Rd. CV2: Cov 6H 19

Highgrove CV4: Westw H 1D 28
  CV22: Bil 4D 44
Highland Rd. CV5: Cov 3B 24
  CV8: Ken 1F 35
Highley Dr. CV6: Cov 4E 19
High Leys, The NN6: Crick 4H 49
High Pk. Cl. CV5: E Grn 1D 22
High St. CV1: Cov 4D 4 (2E 25)
  CV6: Cov 1B 18
  CV8: Ken 3C 34
  CV8: Rytn D 5H 33
  CV12: Bed 4F 7
  CV21: Hillm 3D 46
  CV21: Rugby 6G 41
  NN6: Crick 3H 49
High Vw. Dr. CV7: Ash G 1E 13
Highwayman's Cft. CV4: Canly 1H 29
Hilary Rd. CV4: Canly 6H 23
Hillary Rd. CV22: Rugby 3E 45
Hillcrest Rd. CV22: Bil 2C 44
HILLFIELDS 1G 5 (6G 19)
Hillfields Ho. CV1: Cov 2G 5 (1G 25)
Hillfray Dr. CV3: Cov 1A 32
Hilliard Cl. CV12: Bed 2E 7
HILLMORTON 3E 47
Hillmorton La. CV23: Clift D 1E 47
Hillmorton Rd. CV2: Cov 6C 14
  CV22: Hillm, Rugby 1G 45
Hillmorton Wharf CV23: Hillm 4H 47
Hill Rd. CV7: Ker E 2B 12
Hillside Nth. CV2: Cov 4A 20
Hill St. CV1: Cov 3B 4 (1D 24)
  CV12: Bed 1F 7
  CV21: Rugby 5F 41
Hill Top CV1: Cov 3E 5 (1F 25)
Hilton Cl. CV5: Cov 3B 24
Himbleton Dr. CV3: Bin 2G 27
Himley Rd. CV12: Bed 4B 6
Hinckley Rd. CV2: Walsg S 3G 21
  CV7: Ansty 6H 15
Hinde Cl. CV21: Brow 2A 42
Hipswell Highway CV2: Cov 6D 20
Hiron, The CV3: Cov 4E 25
Hiron Cft. CV3: Cov 4E 25
Hirst Cl. CV23: Long L 4A 40
Hob La. CV8: Burt G 3A 28
Hobley Cl. CV22: Bil 4D 44
Hockett St. CV3: Cov 4F 25
Hocking Rd. CV2: Cov 5D 20
HOCKLEY 6A 16
Hockley La. CV5: E Grn 6A 16
Hodgett's La. CV8: Burt G 1A 28
Hodnet Cl. CV8: Ken 3F 35
Hogan Ho. CV22: Bil 3C 44
Hogarth Cl. CV12: Bed 2E 7
Holbein Cl. CV12: Bed 2E 7
Holborn Av. CV6: Cov 6E 13
Holbrook Av. CV21: Rugby 5G 41
Holbrook La. CV6: Cov 5E 13
  (Beacon Rd.)
  CV6: Cov 2F 19
  (Holbrook Pk. Est., not continuous)
Holbrook Pk. Est. CV6: Cov 2F 19
Holbrook Rd. CV23: Long L 4B 40
HOLBROOKS 5E 13
Holbrook Way CV6: Cov 1F 19
Holcot Leys CV22: Rugby 4G 45
Holland Rd. CV6: Cov 4C 18
Hollicombe Ter. CV2: Cov 2D 20
Hollis La. CV8: Ken 5C 28
Hollis Rd. CV3: Cov 2A 26
Holloway Fld. CV6: Cov 4B 18
Hollow Cres. CV6: Cov 5D 18
Hollowell Way CV21: Brow 2A 42
Hollybank CV5: Cov 4C 24
HOLLYBERRY END 4A 10
Hollybush La. CV6: Longf 4A 14
Holly Dr. CV8: Rytn D 5H 33
Hollyfast La. CV7: Cov 4F 11
Hollyfast Rd. CV6: Cov 3A 18
Holly Gro. CV4: Tile H 2F 23
  CV8: Chu L 4D 38
Hollyhurst CV12: Bed 5D 6
Holly Wlk. CV12: Bed 4G 31
Holmcroft CV2: Walsg S 2F 21
Holme Cl. CV21: Brow 3A 42
Holmes Ct. CV8: Ken 3D 34
Holmes Dr. CV5: E Grn 5B 16
Holmewood Cl. CV8: Ken 3F 35
Holmfield Rd. CV2: Cov 1B 26
Holmsdale Rd. CV6: Cov 3G 19
Holroyd Ho. CV4: Tile H 2D 22
Holy Cross Ct. CV2: Cov 6E 21
Holyhead Rd. CV1: Cov 2A 4 (5G 17)
  CV5: Cov 5G 17
Holyoak Cl. CV12: Bed 5D 6
  CV22: Bil 3C 44
Holywell Cl. CV4: Tile H 3B 22

Homefield La. CV22: Dunc 1D 50
Homeward Way CV3: Bin 3G 27
Honeybourne Cl. CV5: E Grn 1F 23
Honeyfield Rd. CV1: Cov 5F 19
Honeysuckle Cl. CV12: Bed 4B 6
  CV23: Brow 1B 42
Honeysuckle Dr. CV2: Cov 6B 14
Honiley Way CV2: Cov 1D 20
Honiton Rd. CV2: Cov 5B 20
Hood St. CV1: Cov 3G 5 (1G 25)
Hood St. Ind. Est.
  CV1: Cov 3G 5 (1G 25)
Hood's Way CV22: Bil 1D 44
Hope Cl. CV7: Ker E 1C 12
Hopedale Cl. CV2: Cov 1E 27
Hope St. CV1: Cov 4A 4 (2D 24)
Hopkins Rd. CV6: Cov 6C 18
Hopps Lodge Dr. CV21: Rugby 6A 42
Hopton Cl. CV5: E Grn 6E 17
Hornbeam Dr. CV4: Tile H 3B 22
Hornchurch Cl.
  CV1: Cov 6D 4 (3E 25)
Hornchurch Cl. Ind. Est.
  CV1: Cov 6D 4 (3E 25)
Horndean Cl. CV6: Cov 2G 19
Horne Cl. CV21: Hillm 3F 47
Hornets Cl. CV5: Alle 1G 17
Horninghold Cl. CV3: Bin 4E 27
Hornsey Cl. CV2: Cov 3E 21
Horobins Yd. CV12: Bed 1F 7
Horse Shoe Rd. CV6: Longf 4A 14
Horsford Rd. CV3: Cov 6F 25
Horton Cl. CV7: Exh 1H 13
Horton Cres. CV22: Rugby 1G 45
Hosiery St. CV12: Bed 4G 7
Hoskyn Cl. CV21: Hillm 3D 46
Hospital La. CV12: Bed 4A 6
HOSPITAL OF ST CROSS 2H 45
Hotchkiss Way CV3: Bin 5G 27
Hothorpe Cl. CV3: Bin 3F 27
Houldsworth Cres. CV6: Cov 4E 13
Houston Rd. CV21: Rugby 3A 42
How Av. CV5: E Grn 6C 16
Hovelands Cl. CV2: Cov 2C 20
Howard Cl. CV5: Cov 6C 16
Howard St. CV1: Cov 1E 5 (6F 19)
  CV22: Dunc 1D 50
Howat Rd. CV7: Ker E 1B 12
Howcotte Grn. CV4: Tile H 5C 22
Howells Cl. CV12: Bed 5B 6
Howes La. CV3: Finh 4E 31
Howkins Rd. CV21: Rugby 3A 42
Howlette Rd. CV4: Tile H 2C 22
Hudson Rd. CV22: Bil 2E 45
Hudson Va. CV4: Tile H 1A 22
Hugh Rd. CV3: Cov 2A 26
Humber Av. CV1: Cov 6H 5 (3G 25)
  CV3: Cov 3H 25
  (not continuous)
Humber Rd. CV3: Cov 3H 25
Humberstone Rd. CV6: Cov 5C 18
Humphrey Burton's Rd.
  CV3: Cov 4E 25
Humphrey Davy Rd. CV12: Bed 6B 6
Hunters Cl. CV3: Bin 2G 27
Hunters La. CV21: Rugby 4G 41
Hunters La. Ind. Est.
  CV21: Rugby 4G 41
Hunter St. CV21: Rugby 5A 42
Hunter Ter. CV5: Cov 4H 23
Huntingdon Rd. CV5: Cov 3C 24
Hunt Ter. CV4: Canly 5F 23
Hurst Rd. CV6: Longf 4A 14
  CV12: Bed 3F 7
Hurst Wlk. CV6: Longf 4A 14
Hussar Ct. CV3: Cov 4A 26
Hyde Rd. CV2: Cov 6E 21
  CV8: Ken 3D 34
Hypericum Gdns. CV2: Cov 6C 20

Ibex Cl. CV3: Bin 3F 27
Ibstock Rd. CV6: Longf 3A 14
Iden Rd. CV1: Cov 6G 19
Ilam Ct. CV22: Bil 1E 45
Ilam Pk. CV8: Ken 3G 35
Ilford Cl. CV12: Bed 3E 7
Ilford Ct. CV3: Bin W 2B 36
Ilfracombe Gro. CV3: Finh 1C 30
Ilmer Cl. CV21: Brow 2C 42
Ilmington Cl. CV3: Cov 1D 30
Inca Cl. CV3: Bin 4F 27
Inchbrook Cl. CV8: Ken 1G 35

Inchcape Cl. CV22: Caw 3B 44
Independent St. CV23: Kils 5C 48
Ingram Rd. CV5: Cov 4H 23
Innis Rd. CV5: Cov 4A 24
Institute of Creative Enterprise
  CV1: Cov 5E 5
Instone Rd. CV6: Cov 1C 18
International Ho. CV4: Canly 2F 29
Inverary Cl. CV8: Ken 4G 35
Inverness Cl. CV5: E Grn 6E 17
Invicta Rd. CV3: Bin 4F 27
Ireton Cl. CV4: Tile H 3A 22
Ironbridge Way CV6: Longf 2B 14
Ironmonger Row
  CV1: Cov 3D 4 (1E 25)
Irving Rd. CV1: Cov 5H 5 (2G 25)
Isambard Dr. CV6: Longf 3H 13
Ivor Rd. CV6: Cov 6H 13
Ivybridge Rd. CV3: Cov 6F 25
Ivy Farm La. CV4: Canly 6H 23
Ivy Grange CV22: Bil 3C 44
Izod Rd. CV21: Rugby 5F 41

Jack Ball Ho. CV2: Walsg S 1F 21
Jacker's Rd. CV2: Ald G 4B 14
Jacklin Dr. CV3: Finh 2E 31
Jack Martins Halls CV4: Canly 2G 29
Jackson Cl. CV7: Ker E 1C 12
Jackson Gro. CV8: Ken 4G 35
Jackson Rd. CV6: Cov 1F 19
  CV21: Hillm 2E 47
Jackwood Grn. CV12: Bed 6A 6
Jacob Dr. CV4: Canly 6H 23
Jacox Cres. CV8: Ken 3G 35
Jacquard Cl. CV3: Cov 2F 31
Jacquard Ho. CV1: Cov 1H 5 (6G 19)
Jade Cl. CV1: Cov 6F 19
Jaguar Daimler Heritage Trust
  ....1F 17
James Ct. CV21: Rugby 6H 41
  (off James Wlk.)
Jamescroft CV3: W'hall 6E 27
James Dawson Dr.
  CV5: Milli W 2A 16
James Galloway Cl. CV3: Bin 5E 27
James Grn. Rd. CV4: Tile H 2D 22
James Ho. CV2: Cov 2C 20
James St. CV21: Rugby 6H 41
James Wlk. CV21: Rugby 6H 41
Jam Jam Boomerang 3C 32
Jardine Cres. CV4: Tile H 2D 22
Jardine Shop. Cen.
  CV4: Tile H 2D 22
Jasmine Gro. CV3: Cov 4C 26
Jasmine Way CV12: Bed 4B 6
Jasper Cl. CV4: Tile H 1A 22
Jedburgh Gro. CV3: Finh 2C 30
Jefferson Way CV4: Tile H 1A 22
Jeffrey Cl. CV12: Bed 6B 6
Jelliff St. CV2: Cov 2D 22
Jenkins Av. CV5: E Grn 6D 16
Jenkins Rd. CV21: Hillm 2E 47
Jenner St. CV1: Cov 1F 5 (6F 19)
Jephcott Ho. CV1: Cov 2G 5
Jephson Ct. CV2: Ald G 4C 14
Jersey Cl. CV3: Cov 3A 26
Jesmond Rd. CV1: Cov 6H 19
Jim Forrest Cl. CV3: Bin 4F 27
Joanna Dr. CV3: Finh 3E 31
Joan of Arc Ho. CV3: Cov 6G 25
Joan Ward St. CV3: Cov 4F 25
Job's La. CV4: Tile H 1E 23
Jobs Wlk. CV4: Tile H 3E 23
Joe O'Brien Cl. CV3: W'hall 6C 26
Joe Williams Cl. CV3: Bin 4F 27
John Grace St. CV3: Cov 4F 25
John Knight Rd. CV12: Bed 2F 7
John McGuire Cres. CV3: Bin 5E 27
John Nash Sq. CV8: Ken 5D 34
John of Gaunt Ho. CV3: Cov 5G 25
John O'Gaunt Rd. CV8: Ken 5C 34
John Reay Golf Cen. 5A 12
John Rous Av. CV4: Canly 5F 23
John Shelton Dr. CV6: Cov 4E 13
John Simpson Cl. CV8: Wols 6E 37
John Sinclair Ho. CV1: Cov 1D 4
Johnson Av. CV22: Rugby 1D 44
Johnson Rd. CV6: Cov 2A 20
  CV12: Bed 3G 7
John St. CV12: Bed 4E 7
John Thwaites Cl.
  CV22: Rugby 1G 45
John Tofts Ho.
  CV1: Cov 1D 4 (6E 19)
John Wigley Way CV6: Cov 1F 19

Lismore Cft.—Midland Air Mus.

ismore Cft. CV2: Walsg S . . . 3H 21
ITTLE BEDWORTH HEATH . . . 6D 6
it. Church St. CV21: Rugby . . . 6G 41
ittle Cryfield CV4: Canly . . . 4G 29
it. Elborow St. CV21: Rugby . . . 6G 41
ittle Farm CV3: W'hall . . . 1D 32
ittle Flds. CV2: Cov . . . 5A 20
ittle Gro. CV22: Rugby . . . 2A 46
ITTLE HEATH . . . 6H 13
it. Heath Ind. Est. CV6: Cov . . . 6H 13
ITTLE LAWFORD . . . 2H 39
it. Lawford La.
CV21: N'bld A . . . 2G 39
CV23: Lit L . . . 2G 39
it. London La. CV23: Newt . . . 1E 43
it. Orchard Pl. CV22: Bil . . . 2B 44
it. Park St. CV1: Cov . . . 5E 5 (2F 25)
it. Pennington St.
CV21: Rugby . . . 6F 41
it. South St. CV1: Cov . . . 3H 5 (1G 25)
ittlethorpe CV3: W'hall . . . 6D 26
ittleton Cl. CV8: Ken . . . 2E 35
ivingstone Av. CV23: Long L . . . 5H 39
ivingstone Rd. CV6: Cov . . . 3F 19
ivingWell Health Club
Coventry . . . 1H 21
iza Ct. CV21: Brow . . . 1A 42
lamas Farm Ct. CV23: Kils . . . 6C 48
loyd Cres. CV2: Cov . . . 1E 27
loyd Rd. CV21: Brow . . . 3A 42
oach Dr. CV2: Ald G . . . 4B 14
och St. CV3: Cov . . . 3C 26
ocke Cl. CV6: Cov . . . 1C 18
ockhart Cl. CV8: Ken . . . 4E 35
ockhurst La. CV6: Cov . . . 2F 19
ocks, The CV21: Hillm . . . 2F 47
oder Cl. CV4: Tile H . . . 1D 22
odge Rd. CV3: Cov . . . 3B 26
CV21: Rugby . . . 5H 41
ogan Rd. CV2: Cov . . . 3E 21
ole Cl. CV6: Longf . . . 4A 14
ollard Cft. CV3: Cov . . . 4F 25
omsey Cl. CV4: Tile H . . . 3E 23
ondon Rd. CV1: Cov . . . 6G 5 (3G 25)
CV3: Cov, W'hall . . . 6A 26
CV3: W'hall . . . 2D 32
CV8: Rytn D . . . 5H 33
CV23: Dunc, Thurl . . . 4A 50
Long Cl. Av. CV5: Alle . . . 4F 17
Longfellow Ct. CV2: Cov . . . 1C 26
Longfellow Rd. CV2: Cov . . . 1C 26
Longfield Ho. CV6: Cov . . . 2A 20
ONGFORD . . . 4A 14
Longford Bri. Ct. CV6: Longf . . . 3H 13
Longford Rd. CV6: Longf . . . 5H 13
CV7: Exh . . . 2A 14
Longford Sq. CV6: Longf . . . 4H 13
Long Furlong CV22: Rugby . . . 4F 45
Long Hassocks
CV23: Brow, Newt . . . 2H 43
Long La. CV5: Alle . . . 6H 11
CV7: Ker E . . . 6H 11
LONG LAWFORD . . . 5A 40
Longmoor Dr. CV3: Cov . . . 3C 26
Longrood Pl. CV22: Bil . . . 4D 44
Longrood Rd. CV22: Bil . . . 5D 44
Longstork Rd. CV23: Brow . . . 2H 43
Long St. CV12: Bulk . . . 4F 9
Longwood Cl. CV4: Westw H . . . 6D 22
Lonscale Dr. CV3: Cov . . . 1D 30
Lord Lytton Av. CV2: Cov . . . 2D 26
Lord St. CV5: Cov . . . 2B 24
Lorenzo Cl. CV3: W'hall . . . 6D 26
Loudon Av. CV6: Cov . . . 5C 18
Love La. CV8: Ken . . . 2D 34
Lovell Cl. CV7: Exh . . . 6E 7
Lovell Rd. CV12: Bed . . . 3E 7
Loverock Cres. CV21: Hillm . . . 1C 46
Lowercroft CV21: Hillm . . . 3F 47
LOWER EASTERN GREEN . . . 6D 16
Lwr. Eastern Grn. La.
CV5: E Grn . . . 6D 16
Lwr. Ford St. CV1: Cov . . . 4H 5 (2G 25)
(Far Gosford St.)
CV1: Cov . . . 2F 5 (1F 25)
(Perkins St.)
Lwr. Hillmorton Rd.
CV21: Hillm, Rugby . . . 6H 41
Lwr. Holyhead Rd.
CV1: Cov . . . 3B 4 (1D 24)
LOWER LADYES HILLS . . . 2E 35
Lwr. Ladyes Hills CV8: Ken . . . 2E 35
Lwr. Lea Pl. CV21: Hillm . . . 3F 47
Lowe Rd. CV6: Cov . . . 6B 12
Lower Pct. CV1: Cov . . . 3C 4 (1E 25)
Lower Rd. CV7: Barn . . . 2H 15
LOWER STOKE . . . 2A 26
Lower St. CV21: Hillm . . . 2F 47
Loweswater Rd. CV3: Bin . . . 3E 27
Lowfield Rd. CV3: Cov . . . 3C 26
Lowry Cl. CV12: Bed . . . 2E 7
Lowther St. CV2: Cov . . . 6H 19
Loxley Cl. CV2: Cov . . . 6D 14
Loxley Ct. CV2: Cov . . . 6D 14
Lucas Ct. CV21: Rugby . . . 5H 41
Lucerne Cl. CV2: Ald G . . . 5C 14
Lucian Cl. CV2: Walsg S . . . 3H 21
Ludham Pl. CV22: Caw . . . 3A 44
Ludlow Rd. CV5: Cov . . . 2C 24
Luff Cl. CV3: Cov . . . 4B 26
Lulworth Pk. CV8: Ken . . . 2G 35
Lumsden Cl. CV2: Walsg S . . . 2F 21
Lunar Cl. CV4: Canly . . . 1H 29
Lunn Av. CV8: Ken . . . 5C 34
Lunt Roman Fort . . . 3G 31
Lupton Av. CV3: Cov . . . 5E 25
Luscombe Rd. CV2: Cov . . . 2E 21
Luther Way CV5: E Grn . . . 6D 16
Lutterworth Rd. CV2: Cov . . . 5C 20
Luxor La. CV5: Milli W . . . 2A 16
Lydden Cl. CV21: Rugby . . . 3H 41
Lydford Cl. CV2: Cov . . . 3C 20
Lydgate Ct. CV12: Bed . . . 2E 7
Lydgate Rd. CV6: Cov . . . 5D 18
Lymesy St. CV3: Cov . . . 6F 25
Lymington Cl. CV6: Cov . . . 2F 19
Lymington Dr. CV6: Longf . . . 2B 14
Lymore Cft. CV2: Walsg S . . . 2G 21
Lynbrook Rd. CV5: Cov . . . 4H 23
Lynchgate Ct. CV4: Canly . . . 6G 23
Lynchgate Rd. CV4: Canly . . . 6G 23
Lyndale Cl. CV5: Cov . . . 1G 23
(Harewood Rd.)
CV5: Cov . . . 1G 23
(Overdale Rd.)
Lyndale Rd. CV5: Cov . . . 1G 23
Lynden Ho. CV5: Cov . . . 4D 24
Lyndhurst Cl. CV6: Longf . . . 3B 14
Lyndhurst Cft. CV5: E Grn . . . 6A 16
Lyndhurst Rd. CV21: Hillm . . . 3D 46
Lyng Cl. CV5: E Grn . . . 1E 23
Lynmouth Rd. CV2: Cov . . . 2E 21
Lynton Rd. CV6: Cov . . . 1H 19
Lyons Dr. CV5: Alle . . . 1F 17
Lythalls La. CV6: Cov . . . 6F 13
Lythalls La. Ind. Est.
CV6: Cov . . . 1G 19
Lytham Rd. CV22: Bil . . . 2D 44
Lyttleton Cl. CV3: Bin . . . 3G 27

M

Macaulay Rd. CV2: Cov . . . 6D 20
CV22: Rugby . . . 4E 45
Macbeth Cl. CV22: Bil . . . 5E 45
Macdonald Rd. CV2: Cov . . . 1D 26
McDonnell Dr. CV7: Exh . . . 2H 13
Macefield Cl. CV2: Ald G . . . 5D 14
Mackenzie Cl. CV5: Alle . . . 3E 17
McKinnell Cres. CV21: Hillm . . . 1C 46
McMahon Rd. CV12: Bed . . . 6C 6
Madden Pl. CV22: Bil . . . 1C 44
Madeira Cft. CV5: Cov . . . 2A 24
Madison Cl. CV4: Tile H . . . 1A 22
Maffey Ct. CV22: Rugby . . . 1G 45
Magistrates' Court
Coventry . . . 4E 5 (2F 25)
Magnet La. CV22: Bil . . . 3C 44
Magneto Rd. CV3: Cov . . . 3C 26
Magnolia Cl. CV3: Cov . . . 1D 30
Magpie Ho. CV5: E Grn . . . 5B 16
Maguire Ind. Est. CV4: Tile H . . . 4D 22
Maidavale Cres. CV3: Cov . . . 1E 31
Maidenhair Dr. CV23: Brow . . . 1B 42
Main Rd. CV7: Mer . . . 5A 10
CV23: Kils . . . 5B 48
NN6: Crick . . . 2G 49
Main St. CV8: Bran, Wols . . . 4D 36
CV21: N'bld A . . . 2D 40
CV22: Bil . . . 3C 44
CV23: Clift D . . . 4D 42
CV23: Long L . . . 5A 40
CV23: Newt . . . 1E 43
CV23: Thurl . . . 6A 50
Malam Cl. CV4: Tile H . . . 3E 23
Mallard Ct. *CV6: Cov* . . . *3F 19*
(off Gressingham Gro.)
Mallory Way CV6: Longf . . . 3G 13
Mallow Cft. CV12: Bed . . . 4C 6
Mallow Way CV23: Brow . . . 1A 42
Malmesbury Rd. CV6: Cov . . . 6C 12
Malthouse La. CV8: Ken . . . 1C 34
Malt Mill Cl. CV23: Kils . . . 6C 48
Malt Mill Grn. *CV23: Kils* . . . *6C 48*
(off Main Rd.)
Malvern Av. CV22: Rugby . . . 2B 46
Malvern Rd. CV5: Cov . . . 6B 18
Manderley Cl. CV5: E Grn . . . 5A 16
Mandrake Cl. CV6: Cov . . . 4F 13
Manfield Av. CV2: Walsg S . . . 3G 21
Manhattan Way CV4: Tile H . . . 1A 22
Manning Wlk. *CV21: Rugby* . . . *6G 41*
(in Clock Towers Shop. Cen.)
Mann's Cl. CV8: Rytn D . . . 6H 33
Manor Ct. CV8: Ken . . . 2E 35
Manor Est. CV8: Wols . . . 6D 36
Manor Hall M. CV3: W'hall . . . 6D 26
Manor Ho. Cl. CV21: N'bld A . . . 2D 40
Manor Ho. Dr.
CV1: Cov . . . 6C 4 (2E 25)
Manor La. CV23: Clift D . . . 3E 43
Manor Rd. CV1: Cov . . . 6C 4 (3E 25)
CV8: Ken . . . 2D 34
CV21: Rugby . . . 5H 41
CV23: Kils . . . 5C 48
Manor Ter. CV1: Cov . . . 5D 4 (2E 25)
Manor Vw. CV8: Wols . . . 6D 36
Manor Yd. CV1: Cov . . . 5D 4 (2E 25)
Manse Cl. CV7: Exh . . . 5E 7
Mansel St. CV6: Cov . . . 2G 19
Mantilla Dr. CV3: Cov . . . 1C 30
Maple Av. CV7: Exh . . . 5F 7
Maplebeck Cl. CV5: Cov . . . 1C 24
Maple Gdns. CV22: Rugby . . . 2F 45
Maple Gro. CV21: Rugby . . . 5G 41
Maples, The CV12: Bed . . . 4C 6
Mapleton Rd. CV6: Cov . . . 2B 18
Maple Wlk. CV6: Longf . . . 3H 13
Mapperley Cl. CV2: Walsg S . . . 2G 21
March Ct. CV22: Rugby . . . 2G 45
March Way CV3: Bin . . . 5D 26
Mardol Cl. CV2: Cov . . . 3D 20
Margaret Av. CV12: Bed . . . 3E 7
Margeson Cl. CV2: Cov . . . 2E 27
Margetts Cl. CV8: Ken . . . 4D 34
Marie Brock Cl. CV4: Tile H . . . 3F 23
Marina Cl. CV4: Tile H . . . 5C 22
Marion Rd. CV6: Cov . . . 3F 19
Market Cnr. CV8: Bag . . . 4H 31
MARKET END . . . 4B 6
Market End Cl. CV12: Bed . . . 4B 6
Market Harborough Rd.
CV23: Clift D, Newt . . . 1E 43
Market Mall *CV21: Rugby* . . . *6G 41*
(in Clock Towers Shop. Cen.)
Market Pl. CV21: Rugby . . . 6G 41
Market St. CV21: Rugby . . . 5H 41
Market Way CV1: Cov . . . 4C 4 (2E 25)
Marlborough Rd. CV2: Cov . . . 2A 26
CV22: Bil . . . 2E 45
Marlcroft CV3: W'hall . . . 6E 27
Marler Rd. CV4: Tile H . . . 5D 22
Marlow Cl. CV5: Cov . . . 6F 17
Marlston Wlk. CV5: Cov . . . 6F 17
Marlwood Cl. CV6: Longf . . . 4H 13
Marner Cres. CV6: Cov . . . 4D 18
Marner Rd. CV12: Bed . . . 3E 7
Marnhull Cl. CV2: Walsg S . . . 6F 21
Marriner's La. CV5: Cov . . . 5F 17
Marriott Rd. CV6: Cov . . . 6C 18
CV12: Bed . . . 4B 6
Marsh, The NN6: Crick . . . 3H 49
Marshall Rd. CV7: Exh . . . 6D 6
Marshbrook Cl. CV2: Ald G . . . 6D 14
Marsh Cl. NN6: Crick . . . 3H 49
Marshdale Av. CV6: Cov . . . 5G 13
Marshfield Dr. CV4: Canly . . . 4H 29
Marsh Ho. CV2: Walsg S . . . 3G 21
Marsons Dr. NN6: Crick . . . 3H 49
MARSTON . . . 4G 37
Marston Hall Ind. Est.
CV12: Bulk . . . 1B 8
MARSTON JABBETT . . . 1B 8
Marston La. CV12: Bed, Bulk . . . 2F 7
Martin Cl. CV5: E Grn . . . 6C 16
Martindale Rd. CV7: Exh . . . 6G 7
Martin La. CV22: Bil . . . 4D 44
Martins Rd. CV12: Bed . . . 5C 6
Martley Cl. CV3: Bin . . . 2G 27
Marton Ct. CV22: Dunc . . . 4B 44
Martyrs Close, The CV3: Cov . . . 4F 25
Mary Herbert St. CV3: Cov . . . 5F 25
Mary Slessor St. CV3: W'hall . . . 6C 26
Marystow Cl. CV5: Alle . . . 2F 17
Mason Rd. CV6: Cov . . . 1H 19
Masser Rd. CV6: Cov . . . 4E 13
Matlock Cl. CV21: Brow . . . 2A 42
Matlock Rd. CV1: Cov . . . 4F 19
Matterson Rd. CV6: Cov . . . 5C 18
Maudslay Rd. CV5: Cov . . . 2A 24
Maureen Cl. CV4: Tile H . . . 3A 22
Mavor Dr. CV12: Bed . . . 5B 6
Mawnan Cl. CV7: Exh . . . 6F 7
Max Rd. CV6: Cov . . . 5B 18
Maxstoke Cl. CV7: Mer . . . 5A 10
Maxstoke La. CV7: Mer . . . 5A 10
(not continuous)
Maycock Rd. CV6: Cov . . . 3F 19
Mayfield CV12: Bed . . . 3F 7
Mayfield Cl. CV12: Bed . . . 3F 7
Mayfield Dr. CV8: Ken . . . 4G 35
Mayfield Rd. CV5: Cov . . . 4C 24
Mayflower Dr. CV2: Cov . . . 2D 26
May La. CV22: Bil . . . 2D 44
Maynard Av. CV12: Bed . . . 6B 6
Mayo Dr. CV8: Ken . . . 4E 35
Mayor's Cft. CV4: Canly . . . 5F 23
May St. CV6: Cov . . . 2G 19
Meadfoot Rd. CV3: W'hall . . . 6D 26
Mead Gallery . . . *2F 29*
(within Warwick Arts Cen.)
Meadow Community Sports Cen.
. . . 3G 35
Meadowcroft Cl. CV4: Tile H . . . 4D 22
Meadow Furlong CV23: Brow . . . 2H 43
Meadow Ho. CV1: Cov . . . 3A 4 (1D 24)
Meadow Pastures CV22: Caw . . . 2B 44
Meadow Rd. CV6: Cov . . . 4D 12
CV8: Wols . . . 5E 37
CV21: N'bld A . . . 3D 40
Meadow St. CV1: Cov . . . 4A 4 (2D 24)
Meadowsweet CV23: Brow . . . 1A 42
Meadway *CV2: Cov* . . . *4B 20*
(off Beckett Rd.)
Meadway Nth. CV2: Cov . . . 4B 20
Medhurst Cl. CV22: Dunc . . . 2C 50
Medina Rd. CV6: Cov . . . 1G 19
Medland Av. CV3: Finh . . . 1B 30
Melbourne Ct. CV12: Bed . . . 4D 6
Melbourne Rd. CV5: Cov . . . 2C 24
Melford Ct. CV22: Bil . . . 1E 45
Melfort Cl. CV3: Bin . . . 2F 27
Mellish Ct. CV22: Bil . . . 2E 45
Mellish Rd. CV22: Bil . . . 2E 45
Mellor Rd. CV21: Hillm . . . 3F 47
Mellowdew Rd. CV2: Cov . . . 6C 20
Mellowship Rd. CV5: E Grn . . . 5A 16
Melody Cl. CV2: Cov . . . 1C 20
Melrose Av. CV12: Bed . . . 6B 6
Melton Ct. CV22: Caw . . . 3A 44
Melville Cl. CV7: Exh . . . 6E 7
CV22: Bil . . . 2E 45
Melville Rd. CV1: Cov . . . 3A 4 (1C 24)
Memorial Park (Park & Ride) . . . 5C 24
Mercer Av. CV2: Cov . . . 5A 20
Mercer Ct. CV22: Hillm . . . 3D 46
Mercers Mdw. CV7: Ker E . . . 2C 12
Mercia Av. CV8: Ken . . . 4C 34
Mercia Bus. Village
CV4: Westw H . . . 6D 22
Mercia Ho. CV1: Cov . . . 3C 4 (1E 25)
Meredith Rd. CV2: Cov . . . 1D 26
MERIDEN . . . 5A 10
MERIDEN BMI HOSPITAL . . . 4G 21
Meriden Bus. Pk. CV5: Alle . . . 2A 16
Meriden Pk. Homes CV7: Mer . . . 6A 10
Meriden Rd. CV7: Fill . . . 1A 10
Meriden St. CV1: Cov . . . 2A 4 (1D 24)
Meridian Point CV1: Cov . . . 5D 4
Merlin Cl. CV1: Cov . . . 6E 5 (3F 25)
CV23: Brow . . . 1A 42
Merrivale Rd. CV5: Cov . . . 1A 24
Merryfields Way CV2: Walsg S . . . 1F 21
Mersey Rd. CV12: Bulk . . . 4C 8
Merttens Dr. CV22: Rugby . . . 1F 45
Merynton Av. CV4: Canly . . . 6A 24
Meschede Way
CV1: Cov . . . 4E 5 (2F 25)
Meschines St. CV3: Cov . . . 6F 25
Mews, The CV8: Ken . . . 5C 34
CV12: Bed . . . 4F 7
CV21: Hillm . . . 2E 47
Mica Cl. CV21: Rugby . . . 6A 42
Michaelmas Rd. CV3: Cov . . . 3E 25
Michell Cl. CV3: Cov . . . 4B 26
Mickleton Rd. CV5: Cov . . . 3C 24
Middleborough Rd.
CV1: Cov . . . 2A 4 (1D 24)
Middlecotes CV4: Tile H . . . 3F 23
Middlefield Dr. CV3: Bin . . . 3G 27
Middlemarch Bus. Pk.
CV3: W'hall . . . 2C 32
(Siskin Dr.)
CV3: W'hall . . . 5C 32
(Siskin Parkway E.)
Middlemarch Rd. CV6: Cov . . . 4D 18
Middle Ride CV3: W'hall . . . 6D 26
Middlesex Rd. CV3: Cov . . . 3A 26
MIDDLE STOKE . . . 1A 26
Middle St. CV23: Kils . . . 5C 48
Midland Air Mus. . . . 3B 32

A-Z Coventry 61

Midland Rd. CV6: Cov 5G **19**
Midland Trad. Est.
CV21: Rugby 3G **41**
Mile La. CV1: Cov 6E **5** (3F **25**)
CV3: Cov 3F **25**
Miles Mdw. CV6: Cov 1B **20**
Milestone Dr. CV22: Rugby 3F **45**
Milestone Ho. CV1: Cov 4A **4**
Mile Tree La. CV2: Ald G 1F **15**
Milford Cl. CV5: Alle 4F **17**
Millais Cl. CV12: Bed 2E **7**
Millbank M. CV8: Ken 2F **35**
Millbeck CV21: Brow 2B **42**
Millburn Hill Rd. CV4: Canly 6F **23**
Mill Cl. CV2: Ald G 5B **14**
CV8: Wols 6D **36**
Mill Cotts. CV21: Rugby 3B **42**
MILL END 2F **35**
Mill End CV8: Ken 2E **35**
Millennium Way CV8: Wols 6D **36**
Millers Cl. CV22: Dunc 1A **50**
Millers Dale Cl. CV21: Brow 2A **42**
Mill Farm Cl. CV22: Dunc 2C **50**
Millfields Av. CV21: Hillm 3D **46**
Mill Furlong CV23: Brow 2H **43**
Mill Hill CV8: Bag 2F **31**
Mill Ho. Ct. CV6: Cov 3H **19**
Mill La. CV3: Bin 2F **27**
CV12: Bulk 3C **8**
CV23: Clift D 3C **42**
Mill Pk. CV6: Longf 4G **13**
Mill Race La. CV6: Cov 5A **14**
Mill Rd. CV21: Rugby 4A **42**
Mill St. CV1: Cov 1B **4** (1D **24**)
CV12: Bed 3F **7**
Mill Ter. CV12: Bed 1F **7**
Mill Yard, The *CV2: Ald G 5B 14*
(off Egret Wlk.)
Milner Cl. CV12: Bulk 4F **9**
Milner Cres. CV2: Walsg S 1E **21**
Milrose Way CV4: Tile H 4D **22**
Milton Cl. CV12: Bed 5H **7**
Milton St. CV2: Cov 5A **20**
Milverton Rd. CV2: Cov 6C **14**
Minster Rd. CV1: Cov 3A **4** (1D **24**)
Minton Rd. CV2: Walsg S 2F **21**
Miranda Cl. CV3: W'hall 5D **26**
Missing Oak Cl. CV12: Bed 3C **6**
Mistyrose Cl. CV5: Alle 2F **17**
Mitchell Av. CV4: Canly 5E **23**
Mitchell Ct. CV23: Brow 1G **43**
Mitchell Rd. CV12: Bed 4G **7**
Moat Av. CV3: Finh 2B **30**
Moat Cl. CV23: Thurl 6A **50**
Moat Farm Dr. CV12: Bed 6A **6**
CV21: Hillm 4E **47**
Moat Ho. La. CV4: Canly 5G **23**
Moat House Leisure &
Neighbourhood Cen. 1D **20**
Modbury Cl. CV3: Cov 1F **31**
Mohawk Bend CV4: Tile H 1A **22**
Molesworth Av. CV3: Cov 3A **26**
Momus Blvd. CV2: Cov 2C **26**
Monarch Cl.
CV21: Brow, Rugby 2H **41**
Monea Hall CV1: Cov 3G **5**
Monks Cl. CV22: Caw 3A **44**
Monks Croft, The CV3: Cov 5E **25**
Monk's Fld. Cl. CV4: Tile H 3E **23**
Monks Rd. CV1: Cov 4H **5** (2H **25**)
CV3: Bin W 2A **36**
Monks Way NN6: Crick 2H **49**
Monkswood Cres. CV2: Cov 2D **20**
Monmouth Cl. CV5: E Grn 1F **23**
CV8: Ken 2D **34**
Montague Dr. CV23: Kils 5C **48**
Montague Rd. CV22: Bil 6D **44**
Montalt Rd. CV3: Cov 5F **25**
Montbard Cl. CV4: Tile H 3D **22**
Montgomery Cl. CV3: W'hall 2C **32**
Montgomery Dr. CV22: Bil 2C **44**
Monticello Way CV4: Tile H 1A **22**
Montjoy Cl. CV3: W'hall 5D **26**
Montpelier Ho. *CV8: Ken 3D 34*
(off Southbank Rd.)
Montpellier Cl. CV3: Cov 6E **25**
Montrose Rd. CV22: Rugby 2G **45**
Moore Cl. CV6: Longf 4A **14**
Moorfield, The CV3: Cov 4A **26**
Moorings Bus. Park, The
CV6: Longf 2A **14**
Moorlands Av. CV8: Ken 5D **34**
Moorlands Lodge CV8: Ken 5D **34**
Moor's La. CV23: Hillm 3G **47**
Moor St. CV5: Cov 3B **24**
Moreall Mdws. CV4: Canly 3H **29**
Morey St. CV6: Cov 3G **19**
Morfa Gdns. CV6: Cov 5H **17**
Morgan Row CV21: Rugby 1A **46**
Morgans Rd. CV5: E Grn 6A **16**
Morland Cl. CV12: Bulk 4F **9**
Morland Rd. CV6: Cov 6E **13**
Morlay Cl. CV4: Tile H 3E **23**
Morningside CV5: Cov 4D **24**
Morrisania Cl. CV4: Tile H 1A **22**
Morris Av. CV2: Cov 6D **20**
Morris Cl. CV21: N'bld A 3F **41**
Morson Cres. CV21: Hillm 1C **46**
Mortimer Rd. CV8: Ken 6D **34**
Morton Cl. CV6: Cov 1C **18**
Morton Ct. CV21: Hillm 3D **46**
Morton Gdns. CV21: Rugby 1A **46**
Mosedale CV21: Brow 2B **42**
Moseley Av. CV6: Cov 6C **18**
Moseley Rd. CV8: Ken 5F **35**
Moss Cl. CV22: Bil 2E **45**
Mossdale Cl. CV6: Cov 4C **18**
Moss Gro. CV8: Ken 1F **35**
Mottistone Cl. CV3: Cov 6F **25**
Moultrie Rd. CV21: Rugby 1H **45**
Mount, The CV3: Cov 4F **25**
Mountbatten Av. CV8: Ken 4G **35**
Mount Dr. CV12: Bed 3E **7**
Mount Fld. Ct. CV1: Cov 1G **5**
Mount Gdns. CV5: Cov 4D **24**
Mt. Nod Way CV5: E Grn 1E **23**
MOUNT PLEASANT 3E **7**
Mt. Pleasant Rd. CV12: Bed 2E **7**
Mount St. CV5: Cov 2B **24**
Mowbray St. CV2: Cov 1H **25**
Moyeady Av. CV22: Hillm 3C **46**
Moyle Cres. CV5: E Grn 6C **16**
Much Pk. St. CV1: Cov 4E **5** (2F **25**)
Mulberry Ct. CV8: Ken 4D **34**
Mulberry Rd. CV6: Cov 3A **20**
CV22: Bil 1B **44**
Mulliner St. CV6: Cov 5H **19**
Murrayfield Way CV3: Bin 3H **27**
Murrayian Cl. CV21: Rugby 6H **41**
Murray Rd. CV6: Cov 3C **18**
CV21: Rugby 6H **41**
Myers Rd. CV21: Hillm 3G **47**
Mylgrove CV3: Finh 3F **31**
Myrtle Gro. CV5: Cov 3B **24**

N

Nailcote Av. CV4: Tile H 3A **22**
Napier St. CV1: Cov 3H **5** (1G **25**)
Napier St. Ind. Est. CV1: Cov 3H **5**
Napton Ct. CV22: Dunc 5B **44**
Napton Grn. CV5: E Grn 1E **23**
Narberth Way CV2: Walsg S 3F **21**
Nares Cl. CV22: Bil 2E **45**
Narrowboat Cl. CV6: Longf 2B **14**
Naseby Cl. CV3: Bin 4F **27**
Naseby Rd. CV22: Rugby 2A **46**
Nason Gro. CV8: Ken 3F **35**
Naul's Mill Ho.
CV1: Cov 1C **4** (6D **18**)
Navigation Way CV6: Cov 2A **20**
Nayler Cl. CV21: Rugby 3A **42**
Neal Ct. CV2: Walsg S 2G **21**
Neale Av. CV5: Alle 4E **17**
Neale Cl. CV12: Bulk 5E **9**
NEAL'S GREEN 2F **13**
Nelson St. CV1: Cov 1H **5** (6G **19**)
Nelson Way CV22: Bil 2C **44**
Nene Cl. CV3: Bin 5D **26**
Nene Ct. CV23: Long L 5C **40**
Nethermill Rd. CV6: Cov 5C **18**
Newall Cl. CV23: Clift D 4C **42**
New Ash Dr. CV5: Alle 5D **16**
NEW BILTON 6E **41**
Newbold Cl. CV3: Bin 3F **27**
Newbold Footpath
CV21: Rugby 5E **41**
NEWBOLD ON AVON 3F **41**
Newbold Rd.
CV21: N'bld A, Rugby 2E **41**
New Bldgs. CV1: Cov 3D **4** (1F **25**)
Newby Cl. CV3: Cov 6G **25**
New Century Pk. CV3: Cov 3D **26**
Newcombe Cl. CV22: Dunc 2C **50**
Newcombe Rd. CV5: Cov 3B **24**
Newcomen Cl. CV12: Bed 6B **6**
Newcomen Rd. CV12: Bed 5B **6**
Newdigate Cl. CV12: Bed 3E **7**
Newdigate Rd. CV6: Cov 5H **19**
CV12: Bed 2E **7**
Newey Av. CV12: Bed 6B **6**
Newey Dr. CV8: Ken 6E **35**
Newey Rd. CV2: Cov 6D **20**
Newfield Av. CV8: Ken 5F **35**
Newfield Rd. CV1: Cov 5E **19**
Newgate Ct. CV1: Cov 5F **5** (2F **25**)
New Grn. Pk. CV2: Cov 3D **20**
Newhall Rd. CV2: Cov 3D **20**
Newhaven Cl. CV6: Cov 5A **18**
Newington Cl. CV6: Cov 4H **17**
Newland La. CV7: Ash G 1D **12**
Newland Rd. CV1: Cov 5F **19**
Newlands Ct. *CV3: Cov 2H 25*
(off School Cl.)
Newland St. CV22: Rugby 6E **41**
Newman Cl. CV12: Bed 2F **7**
Newmarket Cl. CV6: Ald G 4B **14**
Newnham La.
CV23: Brin, King New 1C **38**
Newnham Rd. CV1: Cov 5H **19**
Newport Rd. CV6: Cov 1F **19**
New Rd. CV6: Cov 1B **18**
CV7: Ash G 2E **13**
Newstead Way CV3: Bin 3H **27**
New St. CV8: Ken 2D **34**
CV12: Bed 4G **7**
CV12: Bulk 4E **9**
CV22: Rugby 6E **41**
NEWTON 1E **43**
Newton Bldgs. CV12: Bed 4F **7**
Newton Cl. CV2: Walsg S 3F **21**
Newton Mnr. La.
CV23: Brow, Newt 1A **42**
Newton Rd.
CV23: Newt, Clift D 1E **43**
Newtown Rd. CV12: Bed 4D **6**
(not continuous)
New Union St.
CV1: Cov 5D **4** (2E **25**)
NHS WALK-IN CENTRE
Coventry 1E **5** (6F **19**)
Rugby 2H **45**
Niagara Cl. CV4: Tile H 1A **22**
Nicholas Cl. CV12: Bed 3G **7**
Nicholas Everton Cl.
CV8: Bran 4E **37**
Nicholls St. CV2: Cov 1H **25**
Nickson Rd. CV4: Tile H 4C **22**
Nightingale Gdns.
CV23: Brow 2G **43**
Nightingale La. CV5: Cov 4H **23**
(not continuous)
Niven Cl. CV5: Alle 4E **17**
Noble Dr. CV22: Caw 3A **44**
Nod Ri. CV5: E Grn 6E **17**
Nolan Cl. CV6: Longf 4F **13**
Nordic Drift CV2: Walsg S 4G **21**
Norfolk St. CV1: Cov 3A **4** (1D **24**)
Norman Ashman Coppice
CV3: Bin W 2A **36**
Norman Av. CV2: Walsg S 1F **21**
Norman Pl. Rd. CV6: Cov 3A **18**
Norman Rd. CV21: N'bld A 3F **41**
Northampton La. CV22: Dunc ...1B **50**
CV23: Dunc 4A **50**
North Av. CV2: Cov 1A **26**
CV12: Bed 4H **7**
Northbrook Rd. CV6: Cov 2H **17**
Northcote Rd. CV21: Rugby 1F **45**
Northey Rd. CV6: Cov 2F **19**
Northfield Rd.
CV1: Cov 5H **5** (2G **25**)
Northfolk Ter. CV4: Canly 5F **23**
North Rd. CV23: Clift D 4D **42**
North St. CV2: Cov 5A **20**
CV21: Rugby 6G **41**
CV23: Kils 5B **48**
Northumberland Rd.
CV1: Cov 3A **4** (1C **24**)
Northvale Cl. CV8: Ken 2F **35**
North Vw. CV2: Walsg S 1G **21**
Northway *CV21: Rugby 6G 41*
(in Clock Towers Shop. Cen.)
Nortoft La. CV23: Kils 3A **48**
Norton Grange CV5: Alle 4G **17**
Norton Hill Dr. CV2: Cov 4E **21**
Norton Leys CV22: Rugby 4F **45**
Norton St. CV1: Cov 2E **5**
Norwich Dr. CV3: Cov 1D **30**
Norwood Gro. CV2: Walsg S 6E **15**
Nova Cft. CV5: E Grn 6A **16**
Nuffield Rd. CV6: Cov 2A **20**
Nuneaton Rd. CV12: Bed 1F **7**
CV12: Bulk 1D **8**
Nunts La. CV6: Cov 5D **12**
Nunts Pk. Av. CV6: Cov 4D **12**
Nutbrook Av. CV4: Tile H 2C **22**

O

Oak Cl. CV8: Bag 4H **31**
CV12: Bed 2G **7**
Oak Ct. CV6: Ker E 2C **1**
Oakdale Ct. CV3: Bin W 1A **3**
Oakdale Rd. CV3: Bin W 2A **3**
Oakey Cl. CV6: Longf 4H **1**
Oakfield Pk. *CV22: Rugby 1F 4*
(off Bilton Rd.
Oakfield Rd. CV6: Cov 5B **1**
CV22: Rugby 1F **4**
Oakford Dr. CV5: Alle 4D **1**
Oakham Cres. CV12: Bulk 4F
Oaklands, The CV4: Tile H 2E **2**
Oaklands Ct. CV8: Ken 6E **3**
Oak La. CV5: Alle 2A **1**
NN6: Crick 2H **4**
Oak La. Pk. Homes CV5: Alle 1B **1**
Oakley Ct. *CV12: Bed 5B*
(off Newcomen Rd.
Oakmoor Rd. CV6: Longf 5A **1**
Oaks, The CV4: Westw H 6E **2**
CV12: Bed 4D
Oak's Pl. CV6: Longf 5A **1**
Oaks Pct. CV8: Ken 5C **3**
Oaks Rd. CV8: Ken 6C **3**
Oak St. CV22: Rugby 1G **4**
Oak Tree Av. CV3: Cov 6C **2**
Oak Tree Rd. CV3: Bin 5G **2**
Oak Way CV4: Tile H 2B **2**
Oakworth Cl. CV2: Walsg S 2F **2**
Oatland Dr. CV22: Caw 2A **44**
Oatlands Cl. CV6: Cov 4E **1**
Oban Rd. CV6: Longf 3H **1**
Oberon Cl. CV22: Bil 5D **44**
Occupation Rd. CV2: Cov 1C **26**
Oddicombe Cft. CV3: Cov 1F **31**
Odeon Cinema
Coventry 3B **4** (2D **24**)
Offa Dr. CV8: Ken 3E **35**
Ofield La. CV23: Kils 5B **48**
Okehampton Rd. CV3: Cov 1G **31**
Okement Gro. CV23: Long L 4B **40**
Olaf Pl. CV2: Walsg S 3G **21**
Old Cathedral 3E **5**
Old Church Rd. CV6: Cov 1H **19**
Old Crown M. CV2: Ald G 4D **14**
Old Farm Cl. CV22: Caw 2B **44**
Oldfield Rd. CV5: Cov 1H **23**
Oldham Av. CV2: Cov 6D **20**
Oldham Way CV23: Long L 5B **40**
Old House La. CV7: Cor 1E **11**
Old Leicester Rd.
CV21: Rugby 2G **41**
(not continuous)
Old Meeting Yd. CV12: Bed 3F **7**
Old Mill Av. CV4: Canly 1H **29**
Old Winnings Rd. CV7: Ker E 2B **12**
Old Yard, The CV2: Walsg S 3F **21**
Olive Av. CV2: Cov 5D **20**
Oliver St. CV6: Cov 4H **19**
CV21: Rugby 6F **41**
Olivier Way CV2: Walsg S 2H **21**
Olton Av. CV5: E Grn 6D **16**
Omar Rd. CV2: Cov 2D **26**
Omega Pl. CV21: Rugby 5H **41**
One O'Clock Ride CV3: Bin W ...2C **36**
Onley La. CV22: Rugby 5A **46**
CV23: Barby 5A **46**
Onley Ter. CV4: Canly 5G **23**
Oratory Dr. CV3: W'hall 6C **26**
Orchard Bus. Pk.
CV21: Rugby 5G **41**
Orchard Ct. CV3: Bin 3G **27**
Orchard Cres. CV3: Cov 4E **25**
Orchard Dr. CV5: E Grn 6A **16**
Orchard La. CV8: Ken 5G **35**
Orchards, The CV23: Newt 1D **42**
Orchard St. CV12: Bed 1F **7**
Orchard Way CV22: Bil 3D **44**
Orchid Cl. CV12: Bed 4C **6**
Orchid Way CV23: Brow 1B **42**
Ordnance Rd. CV6: Cov 5G **19**
Orion Cres. CV2: Walsg S 6E **15**
Orlando Cl. CV22: Bil 5D **44**
Orlescote Rd. CV4: Canly 6H **23**
Ormesby Cl. CV22: Bil 1E **45**
Orpington Dr. CV6: Cov 4F **13**
Orson Leys CV22: Rugby 4F **45**
Orton Rd. CV6: Cov 5E **13**
Orwell Cl. CV23: Clift D 4E **43**
Orwell Rd. CV1: Cov 6H **5** (3H **25**)
Osbaston Cl. CV5: E Grn 6C **16**
Osborne Rd. CV5: Cov 4C **24**
Osbourne Ho. CV1: Cov 5B **4**
Oslo Gdns. CV2: Walsg S 3G **21**
Osprey Cl. CV2: Walsg S 3H **21**
Oswald Way CV22: Rugby 6D **40**
Oswin Gro. CV2: Cov 6C **20**
Othello Cl. CV22: Bil 6D **44**
Otterbrook Ct. CV6: Cov 4D **18**

Oulton Rd.—Rainsbrook Av.

Oulton Rd. CV21: Rugby 3H **41**
Outermarch Rd. CV6: Cov 3E **19**
Outram Av. CV23: Long L 5B **40**
Oval Rd. CV22: Hillm 3B **46**
Overbecks Cl. CV22: Bil 1E **45**
Overberry Cl. CV2: Cov 6D **14**
Overdale Rd. CV5: Cov 1G **23**
OVERSLADE 2E **45**
Overslade Cres. CV6: Cov 3A **18**
Overslade La. CV22: Rugby 4D **44**
Overslade Mnr. Dr.
CV22: Rugby 3F **45**
Over St. CV6: Cov 2A **20**
Owenford Rd. CV6: Cov 2E **19**
Ox Cl. CV2: Cov 4A **20**
Oxendon Way CV3: Bin 3E **27**
Oxford Rd. CV8: Rytn D 4E **33**
Oxford St. CV1: Cov 3H **5** (1G **25**)
CV21: Rugby 6A **42**
Oxley Dr. CV3: Finh 3E **31**

P

Packington Av. CV5: Alle 4F **17**
Packwood Av. CV21: Hillm 3F **47**
Packwood Grn. CV5: E Grn 1E **23**
Paddock, The NN6: Crick 3H **49**
Paddocks, The CV12: Bulk 3D **8**
Paddocks Cl. CV8: Wols 6E **37**
Paddox Cl. CV22: Hillm 3D **46**
Paddox Ct. CV23: Kils 5C **48**
Padstow Rd. CV4: Tile H 4C **22**
Page Rd. CV4: Tile H 5C **22**
Paget Ct. CV2: Ald G 5B **14**
Pailton Cl. CV2: Cov 6C **14**
Pake's Cft. CV6: Cov 5C **18**
Paladine Way CV3: Cov 4A **26**
Palermo Av. CV3: Cov 6F **25**
Palmer La. CV1: Cov 3D **4** (1E **25**)
Palmer's Cl. CV21: Hillm 3F **47**
Palmerston Rd. CV5: Cov 4B **24**
Palm Tree Av. CV2: Cov 6C **14**
Pancras Cl. CV2: Walsg S 1E **21**
Pandora Rd. CV2: Walsg S 2E **21**
Pangbourne Rd. CV2: Cov 2C **20**
Pangfield Pk. CV5: Cov 6G **17**
Pantolf Pl. CV21: N'bld A 2E **41**
Papenham Grn. CV4: Tile H 4E **23**
PARADISE 4H **19**
Paradise St. CV1: Cov 6F **5** (3F **25**)
CV21: Rugby 6A **42**
Paradise Way CV2: Walsg S 1G **21**
Paradise Works CV6: Cov 3H **19**
Paragon Pk. CV6: Cov 4F **19**
Paragon Way CV7: Exh 6F **7**
Parbrook Cl. CV4: Tile H 4C **22**
Park & Ride
Austin Drive 3A **20**
Memorial Park 5C **24**
Park Av. CV6: Cov 5E **13**
Park Cl. CV8: Ken 3F **35**
Park Ct. CV5: Alle 4F **17**
CV21: Rugby 5H 41
(off Park Rd.)
Parkend CV21: Brow 2A **42**
Park Farm Cl. CV22: Bil 1D **44**
Parkfield Dr. CV8: Ken 3F **35**
Parkfield Rd. CV7: Ker E 2C **12**
CV21: N'bld A, Rugby 3D **40**
Parkgate Rd. CV6: Cov 5D **12**
PARK HILL 3G **35**
Park Hill CV8: Ken 3E **35**
Parkhill Dr. CV5: Alle 6D **16**
Park Hill La. CV5: Alle 4E **17**
(not continuous)
Parkland Cl. CV6: Cov 5E **13**
Parklands NN6: Crick 1E **49**
Park Paling, The CV3: Cov 5G **25**
Park Rd. CV1: Cov 6D **4** (3E **25**)
CV8: Ken 2E **35**
CV12: Bed 4F **7**
CV21: Rugby 5G **41**
Parkside CV1: Cov 5E **5** (2F **25**)
Parkside Bus. Pk.
CV1: Cov 6E **5** (3F **25**)
Parkstone Rd. CV6: Cov 6H **13**
Park St. CV6: Cov 3G **19**
Park Vw. CV3: Cov 2B **26**
Parkview Cl. CV7: Exh 1A **14**
Parkview Flats CV5: Cov 4D **24**
Parkville Cl. CV6: Cov 5E **13**
Parkville Highway CV6: Cov 5D **12**
Park Wlk. CV21: Rugby 5G **41**
Parkway CV2: Walsg S 2H **21**
Parkwood Ct. CV8: Ken 3F **35**
Park Wood La. CV4: Tile H 5B **22**
Parnell Cl. CV21: Rugby 6F **41**
Parrotts Gro. CV2: Ald G 3D **14**
Parry Rd. CV2: Cov 3B **20**
Parsons Nook CV2: Cov 5A **20**
Partridge Cl. CV12: Bed 5B **6**
Partridge Cft. CV6: Cov 1A **20**
Passionflower Cl. CV12: Bed 4B **6**
Patricia Cl. CV4: Tile H 3A **22**
Patterdale CV21: Brow 2B **42**
Pauline Av. CV6: Cov 6B **14**
Paul Stacey Ho. CV1: Cov 1G **5**
Pavilion Way CV5: Cov 1B **24**
Paxmead Cl. CV6: Cov 6C **12**
Paxton Rd. CV6: Cov 6C **18**
Paynell Cl. CV6: Cov 6D **12**
Paynes La. CV1: Cov 2H **5** (1H **25**)
CV21: Rugby 6D **40**
Peacock Av. CV2: Walsg S 1F **21**
Pears Cl. CV8: Ken 3D **34**
Pearson Av. CV6: Cov 1B **20**
Pear Tree Cl. CV2: Cov 6B **14**
Pear Tree Way CV22: Bil 2B **44**
Peat Cl. CV22: Bil 2E **45**
Pebblebrook Way CV12: Bed 5G **7**
Pebworth Cl. CV5: E Grn 1F **23**
Peckstone Cl. CV1: Cov 3F **25**
Peel Cl. CV6: Cov 4G **19**
Peel La. CV6: Cov 5H **19**
Peel St. CV6: Cov 4G **19**
Pegmill Cl. CV3: Cov 4H **25**
Pelham Bend CV4: Tile H 1A **22**
Pelham Rd. CV23: Brow 2H **43**
Pembrey Rd. CV21: Rugby 3H **41**
Pembroke Cl. CV12: Bed 5A **6**
Pembrook Rd. CV6: Cov 6E **13**
Pembury Av. CV6: Longf 5A **14**
Penarth Gro. CV3: Bin 5F **27**
Pencraig Cl. CV8: Ken 3G **35**
Pendenis Cl. CV6: Cov 2A **20**
Pendred Rd. CV22: Rugby 6E **41**
Penn Ho. CV4: Tile H 3D **22**
Pennington Ct. CV21: Rugby 6G **41**
Pennington M. CV21: Rugby 6F **41**
Pennington St. CV21: Rugby 6F **41**
Pennington Way CV6: Cov 2G **19**
Penny La. CV22: Hillm 3D **46**
Penny Pk. La. CV6: Cov 5C **12**
Penrith Cl. CV6: Cov 6E **13**
Penrose Cl. CV4: Tile H 5E **23**
Penruddock Dr. CV4: Tile H 5A **22**
Penryhn Cl. CV8: Ken 3G **35**
Pensilva Way CV1: Cov ...1H **5** (6G **19**)
Pepper La. CV1: Cov 4D **4** (2E **25**)
Pepys Cnr. CV4: Tile H 1C **22**
Perchfoot Cl. CV1: Cov 3F **25**
Percival Rd. CV22: Hillm 3B **46**
Percy Cres. CV8: Ken 6C **34**
Percy Rd. CV8: Ken 6C **34**
Percy St. CV1: Cov 3A **4** (1D **24**)
Peregrine Dr. CV5: Alle 5E **17**
Perkins Gro. CV21: Hillm 2D **46**
Perkins St. CV1: Cov 2F **5** (1F **25**)
Permian Cl. CV21: Rugby 3A **42**
Pershore Pl. CV4: Canly 6A **24**
Perth Ri. CV5: E Grn 6E **17**
Peter Ct. CV21: Rugby 6A **42**
Peterlee Wlk. CV2: Walsg S 4G **21**
Peters Wlk. CV6: Longf 4A **14**
Petitor Cres. CV2: Cov 2C **20**
Pettiver Cres. CV21: Hillm 2D **46**
Peveril Dr. CV3: Cov 1C **30**
Peyto Cl. CV6: Cov 6E **13**
Pheasant Cl. CV12: Bed 5B **6**
Pheasant Oak CV4: Tile H 2A **22**
Phillip Docker Ct. CV12: Bulk 4D **8**
Philmont Ct. CV4: Tile H 2A **22**
Phipps Av. CV21: Hillm 2D **46**
(not continuous)
Phoenix Pk. CV7: Exh 1B **14**
Phoenix Way CV2: Cov 1H **25**
CV6: Cov, Longf 4G **13**
CV7: Ash G 4G **13**
Pickard Cl. CV21: Brow 2C **42**
Pickards Way CV7: Exh 2H **13**
PICKFORD 2B **16**
Pickford Grange La. CV5: Alle ...3A **16**
PICKFORD GREEN 3A **16**
Pickford Grn. La.
CV5: Alle, E Grn 5A **16**
Pickford Way CV5: Alle, Cov 4E **17**
Piker's La. CV7: Cor 5E **11**
Pilgrims La. CV23: Newt 1D **42**
Pilgrims Wlk. CV6: Ker E 3C **12**
Pilkington Rd. CV5: Cov 3H **23**
Pilling Cl. CV2: Walsg S 2F **21**
Pilot Cl. CV3: W'hall 1D **32**
Pinders Ct. CV21: Rugby 6H **41**
Pinders La. CV21: Rugby 6H **41**
(not continuous)
Pine Gro. CV21: Hillm 2E **47**
Pines, The CV4: Tile H 5B **22**
CV12: Bed 4C **6**
Pine Tree Av. CV4: Tile H 2E **23**
Pine Tree Ct. CV12: Bed 2G **7**
Pine Tree Rd. CV12: Bed 2H **7**
Pinewood Dr. CV3: Bin W 2A **36**
Pinewood Gro. CV5: Cov 4D **24**
Pinfold St. CV21: Rugby 6E **41**
PINKETT'S BOOTH 1A **16**
PINLEY 5C **26**
Pinley Flds. CV3: Cov 4B **26**
Pinner's Cft. CV2: Cov 5A **20**
Pinnock Pl. CV4: Tile H 3D **22**
Pioneer Ho. CV1: Cov 1G **5**
Pipers Ct. CV3: Finh 2B **30**
Piper's La. CV8: Ken 3E **35**
Pipewell Cl. CV22: Bil 2C **44**
Pipit Wlk. CV23: Brow 2G **43**
Pipkin Ct. CV1: Cov 3F **25**
Placid Cl. CV4: Tile H 1A **22**
Plantagenet Dr. CV22: Bil 5E **45**
Planter Cl. CV22: Caw 3A **44**
Plants Hill Cres. CV4: Tile H 4C **22**
Plexfield Rd. CV22: Bil 2C **44**
Pleydell Cl. CV3: W'hall 1C **32**
Plomer Cl. CV22: Bil 3C **44**
Plowman St. CV21: Rugby 6F **41**
Plymouth Cl. CV2: Cov 3C **20**
Poitiers Rd. CV3: Cov 6F **25**
Polperro Dr. CV5: Alle 5E **17**
Pomeroy Cl. CV4: Tile H 5B **22**
Pond Farm M. CV5: E Grn 5C **16**
Pondthorpe CV3: W'hall 6E **27**
Pontypool Av. CV3: Bin 6F **27**
Pool Cl. CV22: Bil 3D **44**
Poole Rd. CV6: Cov 4B **18**
Poolside Gdns. CV3: Finh 1C **30**
Pope St. CV22: Rugby 6E **41**
Poplar Av. CV12: Bed 4H **7**
Poplar Gro. CV8: Rytn D 5H **33**
CV21: Rugby 5G **41**
Poplar Ho. CV12: Bed 4H **7**
Poplar Rd. CV5: Cov 3B **24**
Poppleton Cl. CV1: Cov ...6A **4** (3D **24**)
Poppy Ct. CV3: W'hall 6D **26**
Poppy Dr. CV23: Brow 1C **42**
Poppyfield Ct. CV4: Canly 3H **29**
Porchester Cl. CV3: Bin 2G **27**
Porlock Cl. CV3: Cov 1G **31**
Porter Cl. CV4: Tile H 4C **22**
Portland Pl. CV21: Rugby 1B **46**
Portland Rd. CV21: Rugby 1B **46**
Portlow La. NN6: Crick 2H **49**
Portree Av. CV3: Bin 2F **27**
Portsea Cl. CV3: Cov 6F **25**
Portway Cl. CV4: Tile H 4C **22**
Portwrinkle Av. CV6: Cov 4A **20**
Postbridge Rd. CV3: Cov 1F **31**
Postle Cl. CV23: Kils 6B **48**
Potlidgate Ct. CV12: Bed 4F **7**
POTTER'S GREEN 1E **21**
Potter's Grn. Rd.
CV2: Walsg S 1E **21**
Potters Rd. CV12: Bed 5C **6**
Potton Cl. CV3: W'hall 6E **27**
Potts Cl. CV8: Ken 4G **35**
Poultney Rd. CV6: Cov 4C **18**
Poundgate La. CV4: Westw H 6B **22**
Powell Rd. CV2: Cov 6A **20**
Powerleague
Coventry 1B **22**
Powis Gro. CV8: Ken 3G **35**
Precinct, The CV1: Cov ...4C **4** (2E **25**)
Prentice Cl. CV23: Long L 4B **40**
Preston Cl. CV4: Tile H 5D **22**
Pretorian Way CV21: Rugby 2G **41**
Pridmore Rd. CV6: Cov 3F **19**
Primary Wlk. CV22: Caw 3A **44**
Primrose Cl. CV23: Brow 1C **42**
Primrose Dr. CV12: Bed 5C **6**
Primrose Hill St.
CV1: Cov 1F **5** (6F **19**)
Prince of Wales Rd. CV5: Cov ...1A **24**
Princes Cl. CV3: Cov 4B **26**
Princes Dr. CV8: Ken 1F **35**
Princes Dr. Ind. Est. CV8: Ken ...6E **29**
Princess Dr. CV6: Cov 1B **20**
Princess St. CV6: Cov 3H **19**
Princes St. CV21: Rugby 5G **41**
Prince Thorpe Ct. CV3: Bin 5E **27**
Princethorpe Way CV3: Bin 5D **26**
Prince William Cl. CV6: Cov 4A **18**
Prior Deram Wlk. CV4: Canly 4F **23**
Prior Pk. Rd. CV22: Bil 1D **44**
Priors, The CV12: Bed 4G **7**
Priorsfield Rd. CV6: Cov 6C **18**
CV8: Ken 1B **34**
Priorsfield Rd. Nth. CV6: Cov ...6C **18**
Priorsfield Rd. Sth. CV6: Cov ...6C **18**
Priors Harnall
CV1: Cov 1G **5** (6G **19**)
Priory Ct. *CV5: Cov 3C 24*
(off Albany Rd.)
Priory Cft. CV8: Ken 4D **34**
Priory Hall CV1: Cov 3E **5** (1F **25**)
Priory Pl. CV1: Cov 3E **5** (1F **25**)
Priory Rd. CV8: Ken 3D **34**
CV8: Wols 5F **37**
Priory Row CV1: Cov 3E **5** (1F **25**)
Priory St. CV1: Cov 4E **5** (1F **25**)
Priory Theatre 3D **34**
Priory Vis. Cen. 3E **5**
Privet Rd. CV2: Cov 6B **14**
Proffitt Av. CV6: Cov 1A **20**
Progress Cl. CV3: Bin 5G **27**
Progress Way CV3: Bin 4G **27**
Projects Dr. CV21: Rugby 3H **41**
Prologis Pk. CV6: Ker E 3C **12**
(not continuous)
Prospect Pk. CV21: Rugby 1G **41**
Prospect Way CV21: Rugby 4A **42**
Providence St. CV5: Cov 4B **24**
Pudding Bag La. CV23: Thurl 6A **50**
Puma Way CV1: Cov 6E **5** (3F **25**)
Pumphouse Cl. CV6: Longf 2B **14**
Purcell Rd. CV6: Cov 2B **20**
Purefoy Rd. CV3: Cov 4F **25**
Purlieu La. CV8: Ken 3B **34**
Pyke Way NN6: Crick 2H **49**
Pytchley Rd. CV22: Rugby 2A **46**
Pyt Pk. CV5: Cov 6H **17**

Q

Quadrant, The
CV1: Cov 5C **4** (2E **25**)
Quarry Cl. CV21: N'bld A 2F **41**
Quarryfield La.
CV1: Cov 6G **5** (3G **25**)
CV3: Cov 3G **25**
Quarry Rd. CV8: Ken 2C **34**
Quarrywood Gro. CV2: Cov 6A **20**
Queen Isabel's Av. CV3: Cov 4F **25**
Queen Margaret's Rd.
CV4: Canly 4F **23**
Queen Mary's Rd. CV6: Cov 2F **19**
CV12: Bed 1G **7**
Queen Philippa St. CV3: Cov 6F **25**
Queen's Cl. CV8: Ken 5D **34**
Queensferry Cl. CV22: Bil 3C **44**
Queensland Av. CV5: Cov 2B **24**
Queensland Gdns. CV12: Bed 4D **6**
Queens Rd. CV1: Cov 5B **4** (2D **24**)
CV8: Ken 5D **34**
CV23: Bret 2H **37**
Queen St. CV12: Bed 4G **7**
Queenswood Ct. CV7: Ker E 4H **11**
Queen Victoria Rd.
CV1: Cov 3C **4** (1D **24**)
(not continuous)
Queen Victoria St.
CV21: Rugby 6A **42**
Quilletts Cl. CV6: Cov 1A **20**
Quinn Cl. CV3: Cov 5B **26**
Quinton Lodge CV3: Cov 5F **25**
Quinton Pde. CV3: Cov 5F **25**
Quinton Pk. CV3: Cov 5F **25**
Quinton Rd. CV1: Cov 6E **5** (3F **25**)
CV3: Cov 4F **25**
Quorn Way CV3: Bin 4E **27**

R

Rabbit La. CV12: Bed 2A **6**
Radcliffe Rd. CV5: Cov 4B **24**
RADFORD 3D **18**
Radford Circ. CV6: Cov 6D **18**
Radford Ho. CV6: Cov 3C **18**
Radford Rd. CV1: Cov 1C **4** (6E **19**)
CV6: Cov 3C **18**
Radnor Wlk. CV2: Walsg S 2F **21**
Raffles Pl. CV23: Long L 5B **40**
Raglan Ct. CV1: Cov 2H **5** (1G **25**)
Raglan Gro. CV8: Ken 3F **35**
Raglan Ho. CV1: Cov 2G **5** (1G **25**)
Raglan St. CV1: Cov 3G **5** (1G **25**)
Railings, The CV21: Rugby 5H **41**
Railport App. NN6: Crick 2D **48**
Railway St. CV23: Long L 5A **40**
Railway Ter. CV12: Bed 4G **7**
CV21: Rugby 6H **41**
RAINSBROOK 5A **46**
Rainsbrook Av. CV22: Hillm 3C **46**

A-Z Coventry 63

Raleigh Rd.—Sandilands Cl.

Raleigh Rd. CV2: Cov 1B 26
Ralph Rd. CV6: Cov 5B 18
Ramsay Cres. CV5: Alle 3F 17
Ranby Rd. CV2: Cov 6H 19
Randall Rd. CV8: Ken 5D 34
Randle St. CV6: Cov 5C 18
Rangemoor CV3: W'hall 6D 26
Rankine Cl. CV21: N'bld A 2D 40
Rannock Cl. CV3: Bin 2G 27
Ransom Rd. CV6: Cov 2G 19
Ranulf Cft. CV3: Cov 5E 25
Ranulf St. CV3: Cov 5E 25
Raphael Cl. CV5: Cov 1G 23
Rathbone Cl. CV7: Ker E 2B 12
CV21: Hillm 3E 47
Ratliffe Rd. CV22: Rugby 4F 45
Raven Cragg Rd. CV5: Cov 4A 24
Ravenglass CV21: Brow 2B 42
Ravensdale Rd. CV2: Cov 1C 26
Ravensholst CV4: Canly 6H 23
Ravensthorpe Cl. CV3: Bin 4E 27
Rawnsley Dr. CV8: Ken 3F 35
Raymond Cl. CV6: Longf 3H 13
Raynor Cres. CV12: Bed 5B 6
Reading Cl. CV2: Ald G 5B 14
Read St. CV1: Cov 3H 5 (1G 25)
Read St. Ind. Est.
CV1: Cov 3H 5 (1G 25)
Recreation Rd. CV6: Cov 5A 14
Rectory Cl. CV5: Alle 4G 17
CV7: Exh 5E 7
NN6: Crick 3H 49
Rectory Dr. CV7: Exh 5E 7
Rectory La. CV5: Alle 4G 17
Redcap Cft. CV6: Cov 4F 13
Redcar Rd. CV1: Cov 5G 19
Redditch Wlk.
CV2: Walsg S 3G 21
Redesdale Av. CV6: Cov 6B 18
Redfern Av. CV8: Ken 2E 35
Redgrave Cl. CV2: Walsg S 2H 21
Redhill Rd. CV23: Long L 5B 40
Redland Cl. CV2: Ald G 6E 15
Redland La. CV8: Rytn D 4G 33
Red La. CV6: Cov 5G 19
CV8: Burt G 2A 28
Red La. Ind. Est. CV6: Cov 4H 19
Red Lodge Dr. CV22: Bil 3E 45
Red Poll Rd. CV21: Rugby 5A 42
Redruth Cl. CV6: Cov 2A 20
Redthorne Gro. CV8: Ken 6F 29
Rees Dr. CV3: Finh 2E 31
Reeve Dr. CV8: Ken 4E 35
Regency Ct. CV5: Cov 4B 24
Regency Dr. CV3: Finh 1B 30
CV8: Ken 5D 34
Regent Pl. CV21: Rugby 5G 41
Regent St. CV1: Cov 6A 4 (3D 24)
CV12: Bed 2G 7
CV21: Rugby 6G 41
Regiment Ct. CV6: Cov 1C 18
Regina Cres. CV2: Walsg S 3G 21
Regis Wlk. CV2: Walsg S 3F 21
Relton M. CV6: Cov 4H 19
Rembrandt Cl. CV5: Cov 1G 23
Remembrance Rd.
CV3: W'hall 6D 26
Renfrew Wlk. CV4: Tile H 4E 23
Renison Rd. CV12: Bed 5C 6
Renolds Cl. CV4: Cov 2G 23
Renown Av. CV5: Cov 3G 23
Repton Dr. CV6: Cov 6B 14
Reservoir Rd. CV21: Rugby 3A 42
Rex Cl. CV4: Tile H 4B 22
Reynolds Cl. CV21: Hillm 3F 47
Reynolds Rd. CV12: Bed 2E 7
Ribble Cl. CV12: Bulk 4D 8
Ribble Rd. CV3: Cov 2H 25
Richard Joy Cl. CV6: Cov 6E 13
Richards Cl. CV8: Ken 3D 34
Richardson Way
CV2: Walsg S 2H 21
Richmond Rd. CV21: Rugby 1A 46
Richmond St. CV2: Cov 1A 26
Ricoh Arena 5G 13
Ricoh Arena Station (Rail) 5G 13
Riddings, The CV5: Cov 5H 23
Ridefort Cl. CV4: Tile H 3E 23
Ridge Ct. CV5: Alle 4E 17
Ridge Dr. CV21: Rugby 5B 42
Ridgethorpe CV3: W'hall 1E 33
Ridgeway Av. CV3: Cov 6E 25
Ridgley Rd. CV4: Tile H 3C 22
Rigdale Cl. CV2: Cov 2E 27
Riley Cl. CV8: Ken 4G 35
Riley Ct. CV21: Rugby 6A 42
Riley Ho. CV1: Cov 5D 4 (2E 25)
Riley Sq. CV2: Cov 1B 20
Ringway Hill Cross
CV1: Cov 3B 4 (1D 24)
Ringway Queens
CV1: Cov 5B 4 (2D 24)
Ringway Rudge
CV1: Cov 4B 4 (2D 24)
Ringway St Johns
CV1: Cov 5E 5 (2F 25)
Ringway St Nicholas
CV1: Cov 2C 4 (1E 25)
Ringway St Patrick's
CV1: Cov 6D 4 (3E 25)
Ringway Swanswell
CV1: Cov 2E 5 (1F 25)
Ringway Whitefriars
CV1: Cov 3F 5 (2F 25)
Ringwood Highway
CV2: Walsg S 6E 15
Ripon Cl. CV5: Alle 2E 17
Risborough Cl. CV5: Cov 1G 23
River Cl. CV12: Bed 5D 6
River Ct. CV1: Cov 3A 4 (1D 24)
Riverford Cft. CV4: Canly 2H 29
Riverside Cl. CV3: Cov 5H 25
Riverslea Rd. CV3: Cov 3C 26
River Wlk. CV2: Cov 6C 14
Roadway Cl. CV12: Bed 4F 7
Robbins Ct. CV22: Hillm 3D 46
Robert Atchinson Way
CV7: Ker E 2B 12
(off Coopers Mdw.)
Robert Cl. CV3: W'hall 2C 32
Robert Cramb Av. CV4: Tile H 4D 22
Robert Hill Cl. CV21: Hillm 2E 47
Robert Mounford Way
CV4: Tile H 4D 22
Robert Rd. CV7: Exh 6D 6
Robertson Cl. CV23: Clift D 4E 43
Robin Hood Rd. CV3: W'hall 6C 26
Robinson Rd. CV12: Bed 6B 6
Robotham Cl. CV21: N'bld A 3F 41
Rocheberie Way CV22: Rugby 3F 45
Rochester Rd. CV5: Cov 4A 24
Rock Cl. CV6: Cov 1B 20
Rocken End CV6: Cov 2F 19
Rock Farm La. CV8: Bag 6H 31
Rock La. CV7: Cor 1G 11
Rocky La. CV8: Ashow, Ken 5G 35
Rodhouse Cl. CV4: Tile H 3B 22
Rodney Cl. CV22: Bil 2C 44
Rodway Dr. CV5: E Grn 6B 16
Rodyard Way CV1: Cov 6F 5 (3F 25)
Roisins Vineyard CV12: Bed 4B 6
Rokeby Ct. CV22: Rugby 4F 45
Rokeby St. CV21: Rugby 6B 42
Roland Av. CV6: Cov 5D 12
Roland Mt. CV6: Cov 5E 13
Rollason Cl. CV6: Cov 2E 19
Rollason Rd. CV6: Cov 2D 18
Rollasons Yd. CV6: Cov 5A 14
Roman Rd. CV2: Cov 1B 26
Roman Way CV3: Finh 3F 31
CV21: Rugby 2G 41
Romford Rd. CV6: Cov 6D 12
Romney Pl. CV22: Rugby 4F 45
Romsley Rd. CV6: Cov 4E 19
Romulus Wlk. CV4: Tile H 1A 22
Ro-Oak Rd. CV6: Cov 5B 18
Rookery La. CV6: Cov 4D 12
Roosevelt Dr. CV4: Tile H 2C 22
Rootes Halls CV4: Canly 2G 29
Roper Cl. CV21: Hillm 3E 47
Rosaville Cres. CV5: Alle 4E 17
Rose Av. CV6: Cov 5B 18
Roseberry Av. CV2: Cov 1B 20
Rose Cott. Flats CV5: E Grn 5B 16
Rose Cft. CV8: Ken 2C 34
Rosegreen Cl. CV3: Cov 6G 25
Rosehip Dr. CV2: Cov 4B 20
Roseland Rd. CV8: Ken 5D 34
Roselands Av. CV2: Cov 2D 20
Rosemary Cl. CV4: Tile H 1C 22
Rosemary Hill CV8: Ken 3D 34
Rosemary M. CV8: Ken 3D 34
Rosemount Cl. CV2: Cov 3E 21
Rosemullion Cl. CV7: Exh 6F 7
Rosewood Av. CV22: Rugby 3G 45
Ross Cl. CV5: E Grn 5B 16
Ross Ct. CV21: Rugby 6B 42
Rosslyn Av. CV6: Cov 4A 18
Rotherham Cl. CV22: Caw 3A 44
Rotherham Rd. CV6: Cov 6D 12
Rothesay Av. CV4: Tile H 2F 23
Rothley Dr. CV21: Brow 2C 42
Roughknowles Rd.
CV4: Westw H 6B 22
Rouncil La. CV8: Ken 6C 34
Round Av. CV23: Long L 4A 40
Round Ho. Rd. CV3: Cov 4A 26
Rounds Gdns. CV21: Rugby 6F 41
Rounds Hill CV8: Ken 6C 34
Round St. CV21: Rugby 6F 41
Rover Rd. CV1: Cov 4C 4 (2E 25)
Row, The CV8: Bag 4H 31
Rowan Cl. CV3: Bin W 2B 36
Rowan Dr. CV22: Bil 1B 44
Rowan Gro. CV2: Walsg S 6E 15
Rowan Ho. CV4: Westw H 6D 22
Rowans, The CV12: Bed 4C 6
Rowcroft Rd. CV2: Walsg S 4G 21
Rowe Cl. CV21: Hillm 3G 47
Rowington Cl. CV6: Cov 5H 17
Rowland St. CV21: Rugby 6F 41
Rowley Dr. CV3: W'hall 2B 32
Rowley La. CV3: W'hall 3D 32
Rowley Rd. CV3: W'hall 3H 31
CV8: Bag 3H 31
ROWLEYS GREEN 4G 13
Rowley's Grn. CV6: Longf 4G 13
Rowleys Grn. Ind. Est.
CV6: Longf 4G 13
Rowley's Grn. La. CV6: Longf 4G 13
Rowse Cl. CV21: Brow 2A 42
Royal Ct. CV21: Rugby 6F 41
Royal Cres. CV3: W'hall 1C 32
Royal Oak La. CV7: Ash G 1E 13
CV12: Bed 1E 13
Royal Oak Yd. CV12: Bed 2F 7
Royston Cl. CV3: Bin 1G 27
Rubens Cl. CV5: Cov 1G 23
Rudgard Rd. CV6: Longf 4A 14
Rudge Rd. CV1: Cov 4B 4 (2D 24)
RUGBY 6G 41
Rugby Art Gallery & Museum 6G 41
Rugby Golf Course 5C 42
RUGBY MYTON DAY HOSPICE
2H 45
Rugby Rd. CV3: Bin W 4H 27
CV8: Bran 4H 27
CV8: Wols 5G 37
CV12: Bulk 4F 9
CV22: Dunc 2D 50
CV23: Chu L 4E 39
CV23: Clift D 3F 43
(Lilbourne Rd.)
CV23: Clift D 4D 42
(Station Rd.)
CV23: Harb M, Harb P 1C 40
CV23: Kils 5H 47
CV23: Long L 5B 40
Rugby RUFC 1E 45
Rugby School Sports Cen. 1H 45
Rugby Station (Rail) 5A 42
Rugby Theatre 6G 41
Rugby Western Relief Rd.
CV21: N'bld A, Rugby 6C 40
CV23: Caw, Law H, Long L
2A 44
Runcorn Wlk. CV2: Walsg S 3G 21
Rupert Brooke Rd.
CV22: Rugby 4E 45
Rupert Rd. CV6: Cov 2D 18
Rushall Path CV4: Canly 5F 23
Rushmoor Dr. CV5: Cov 1B 24
Ruskin Cl. CV6: Cov 4H 17
CV22: Rugby 5F 45
Russell Av. CV22: Dunc 1D 50
Russell St. CV1: Cov 1E 5 (6F 19)
Russell St. Nth. CV1: Cov 6F 19
Russelsheim Way
CV22: Rugby 1G 45
Russet Gro. CV4: Canly 3H 29
Rutherglen Av. CV3: Cov 6A 26
Rutland Cl. CV21: Hillm 1C 46
Rutland Cft. CV3: Bin 4F 27
Rydal Cl. CV5: Alle 2F 17
CV21: Brow 3B 42
Rye Cl. CV22: Dunc 2C 50
Rye Hill CV5: Alle 4E 17
Rye Hill Office Pk. CV5: Alle 3E 17
Rye Piece CV12: Bed 4G 7
Rye Piece Ringway CV12: Bed 3F 7
Ryhope Cl. CV12: Bed 5A 6
Ryley St. CV1: Cov 3B 4 (1E 25)
Rylston Av. CV6: Cov 1C 18
RYTON 4F 9
Ryton Cl. CV4: Canly 4F 23
RYTON-ON-DUNSMORE 5H 33

S

Sackville Ho. CV1: Cov 1G 5
Saddington Rd. CV3: Bin 4E 27
Sadler Gdns. CV12: Bed 4G 7
Sadler Rd. CV6: Cov 1C 18
Saffron Cl. CV23: Brow 1C 42
St Agatha's Rd. CV2: Cov 1A 26
St Andrews Ct. CV21: Rugby 5G 41
St Andrews Cres.
CV22: Rugby 3G 45
St Andrew's Rd. CV5: Cov 4B 24
St Anne's Rd. CV22: Bil 2E 45
St Ann's Rd. CV2: Cov 1A 26
St Augustine's Wlk. CV6: Cov 3C 18
St Austell Rd. CV2: Cov 1E 27
St Bartholomews Cl. CV3: Bin 2G 27
St Bernards Wlk. CV3: W'hall 6D 26
St Catherine's Cl. CV3: Cov 4B 26
St Catherines Lodge CV6: Cov 6C 18
St Christian's Cft. CV3: Cov 4F 25
St Christian's Rd. CV3: Cov 4G 25
St Clements Ct. CV2: Cov 2D 20
St Columba's Cl.
CV1: Cov 1C 4 (6E 19)
St Davids Orchard CV3: Bin 5F 27
St Elizabeth's Rd. CV6: Cov 3G 19
St Georges Av. CV22: Rugby 2G 45
St George's Rd. CV1: Cov 2H 25
St Giles Rd. CV7: Ash G 2F 13
St Helen's Way CV5: Alle 2F 17
St Ives Rd. CV2: Cov 1D 26
St James Ct. CV3: W'hall 6E 27
St James Gdns. CV12: Bulk 4E 9
St James La. CV3: W'hall 1C 32
ST JOHNS 6D 34
St Johns Av. CV8: Ken 5D 34
CV22: Hillm 3C 46
St Johns Flats CV8: Ken 5E 35
St John's La. CV23: Long L 4A 40
St John's St. CV1: Cov 5E 5 (2F 25)
CV8: Ken 5E 35
St John St. CV21: Rugby 5G 41
St Jude's Cres. CV3: W'hall 5D 26
St Just's Rd. CV2: Cov 6F 21
St Lawrence's Rd. CV6: Cov 1H 19
St Leonard's Wlk.
CV8: Rytn D 5G 33
St Luke's Rd. CV6: Cov 5F 13
St Margaret Rd. CV1: Cov 2H 25
St Margarets Av. CV8: Wols 5E 37
St Mark's Av. CV22: Bil 4C 44
St Mark's Ct. CV22: Bil 3D 44
St Martin's Rd. CV3: Finh 2E 31
(not continuous)
St Mary's Ct. CV8: Ken 5D 34
St Mary's Guildhall *4E 5*
(off Bayley La.)
St Mary St. CV1: Cov 4E 5 (2F 25)
St Matthews St.
CV21: Rugby 6G 41
St Michael's Av. CV1: Cov 3E 5
St Michael's Rd. CV2: Cov 1A 26
St Nicholas Av. CV8: Ken 5D 34
St Nicholas Cl. CV1: Cov 5E 19
St Nicholas Ct. CV6: Cov 4D 18
(Dugdale Rd.)
CV6: Cov 3H 19
(Torcastle Cl.)
St Nicholas St.
CV1: Cov 1C 4 (5E 19)
St Osburg's Rd. CV2: Cov 1A 26
St Patricks Rd.
CV1: Cov 6D 4 (2E 25)
St Paul's Rd. CV6: Cov 4G 19
St Peter's Ct. CV1: Cov 1G 5
St Peter's Rd. CV21: Rugby 1A 46
St Thomas' Ct.
CV1: Cov 5A 4 (2D 24)
St Thomas Ho. CV1: Cov 5A 4
St Thomas Rd. CV6: Cov 5A 14
Salcombe Cl. CV3: W'hall 6D 26
Salemorton Ct. CV22: Dunc 5B 44
Salford Cl. CV2: Cov 5A 20
Salisbury Av. CV3: Cov 6E 25
Salisbury Cl. CV8: Wols 6D 36
Salt La. CV1: Cov 4D 4 (2E 25)
Salvia Way CV12: Bed 4B 6
Sam Gault Cl. CV3: Bin 5F 27
Sammons Way CV4: Tile H 3B 22
Sampson Cl. CV2: Cov 1C 20
Samuel Hayward Ho.
CV2: Cov 1B 20
(off Roseberry Av.)
Samuel Rd. CV2: Cov 4B 20
Samuel Va. Ho.
CV1: Cov 1C 4 (6E 19)
Sandby Cl. CV12: Bed 2E 7
Sanders Rd. CV6: Longf 2B 14
Sandford Cl. CV2: Ald G 5D 14
Sandford Way CV22: Dunc 2C 50
Sandgate Cres. CV2: Cov 2E 27
Sandhurst Gro. CV6: Cov 5D 18
Sandilands Cl. CV2: Cov 6E 21

X

Y

MIX

Paper from
responsible sources

FSC® C021017

www.fsc.org

SAFETY CAMERA INFORMATION

PocketGPSWorld.com's CamerAlert is a self-contained speed and red light camera warning system for SatNavs and Android or Apple iOS smartphones/tablets. Visit www.cameralert.co.uk to download.

Safety camera locations are publicised by the Safer Roads Partnership which operates them in order to encourage drivers to comply with speed limits at these sites. It is the driver's absolute responsibility to be aware of and to adhere to speed limits at all times.

By showing this safety camera information it is the intention of Geographers' A-Z Map Company Ltd., to encourage safe driving and greater awareness of speed limits and vehicle speed. Data accurate at time of printing.

Printed and bound in the United Kingdom by Gemini Press Ltd., Shoreham-by-Sea, West Sussex
Printed on materials from a sustainable source